LARGE PRINT
Bold and Easy

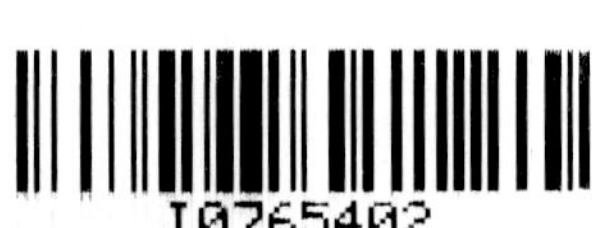

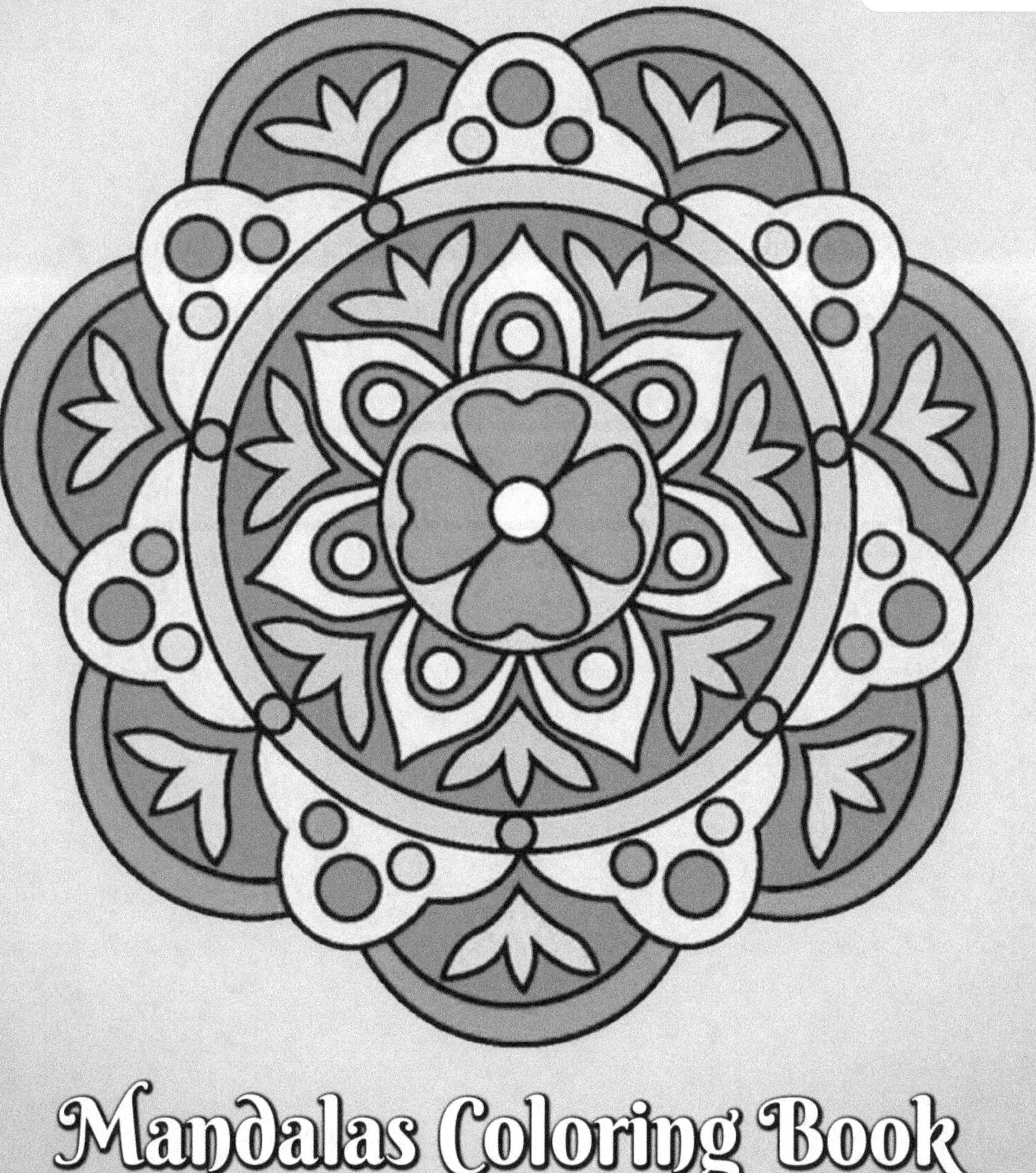

Mandalas Coloring Book

this book belongs to

____

____

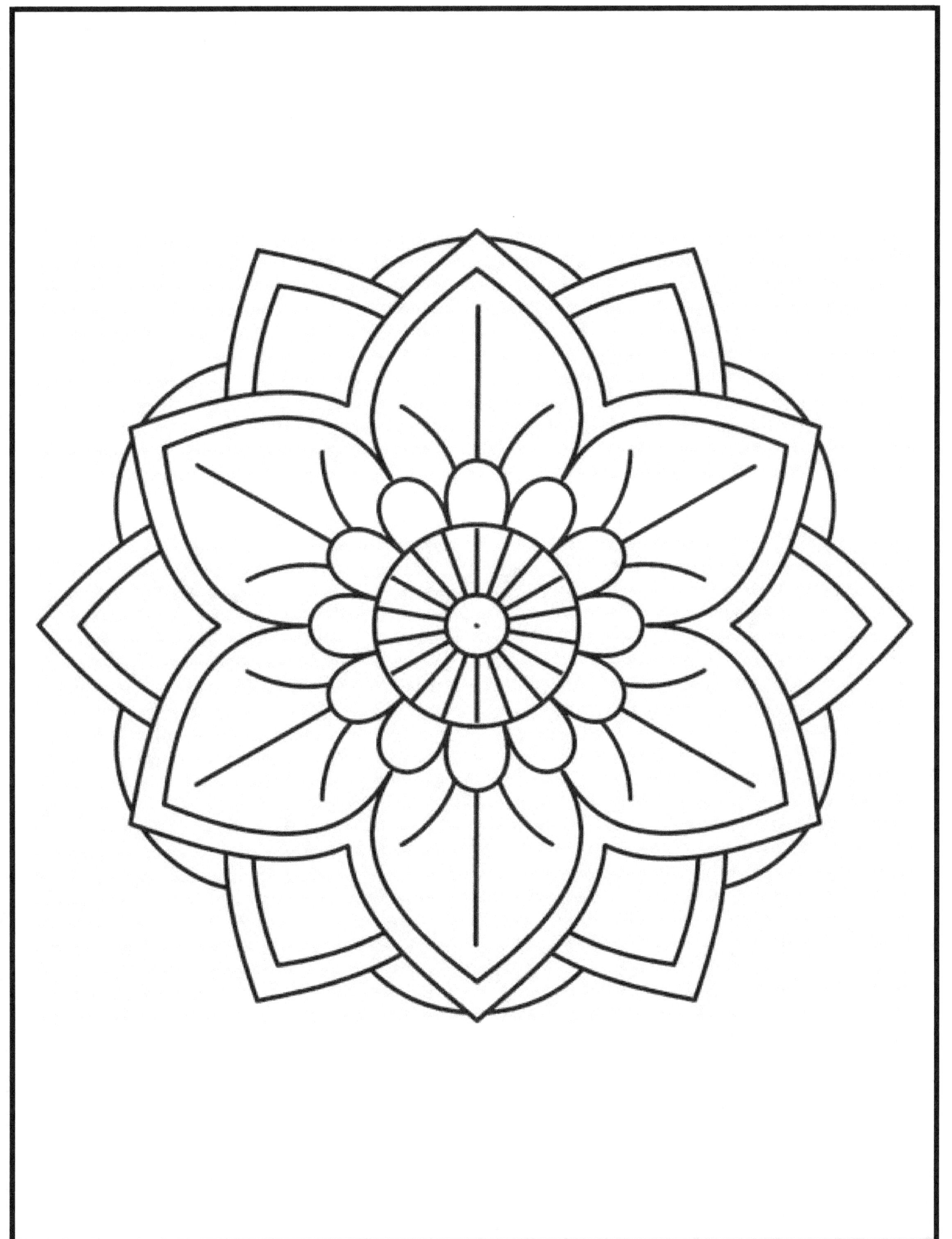

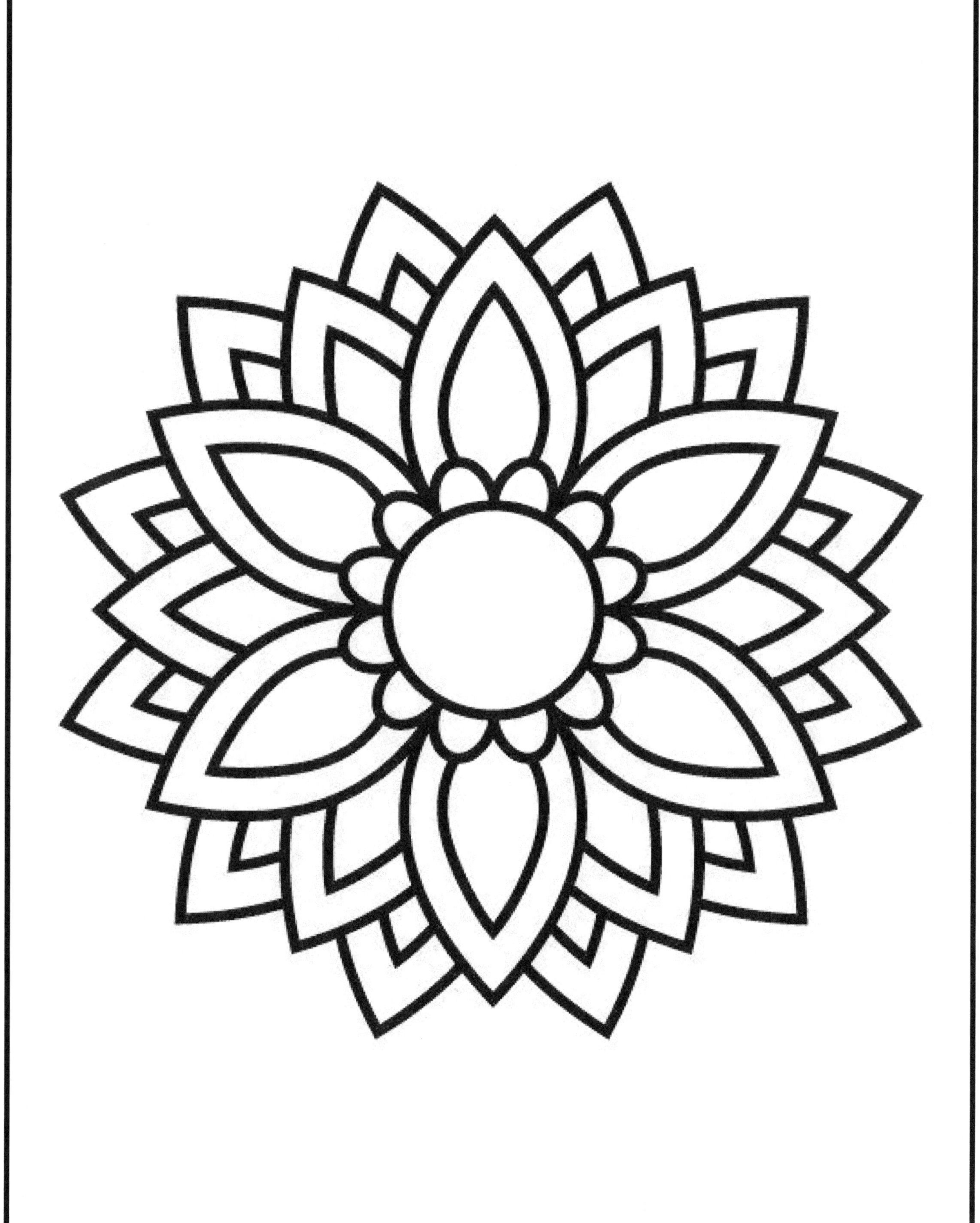

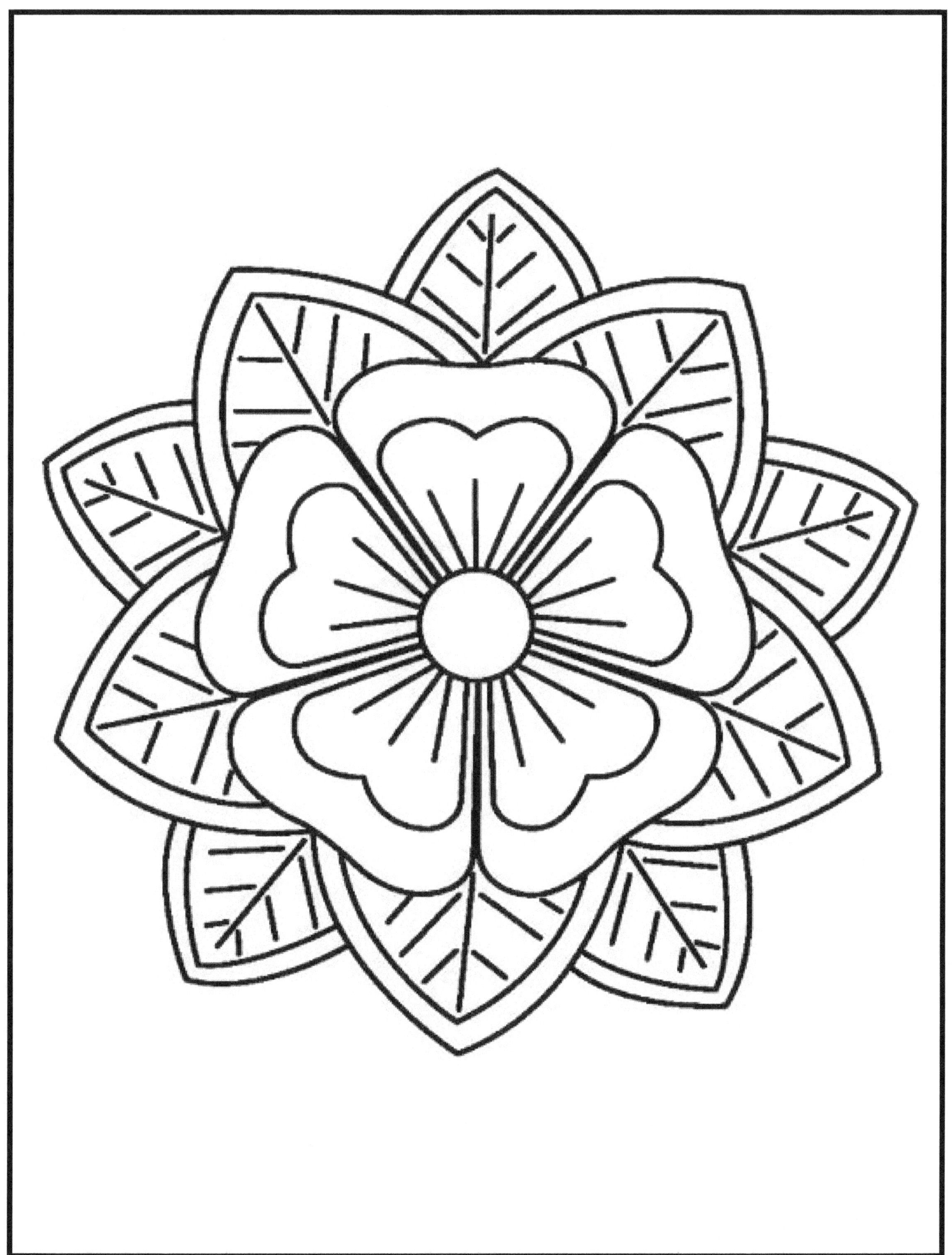

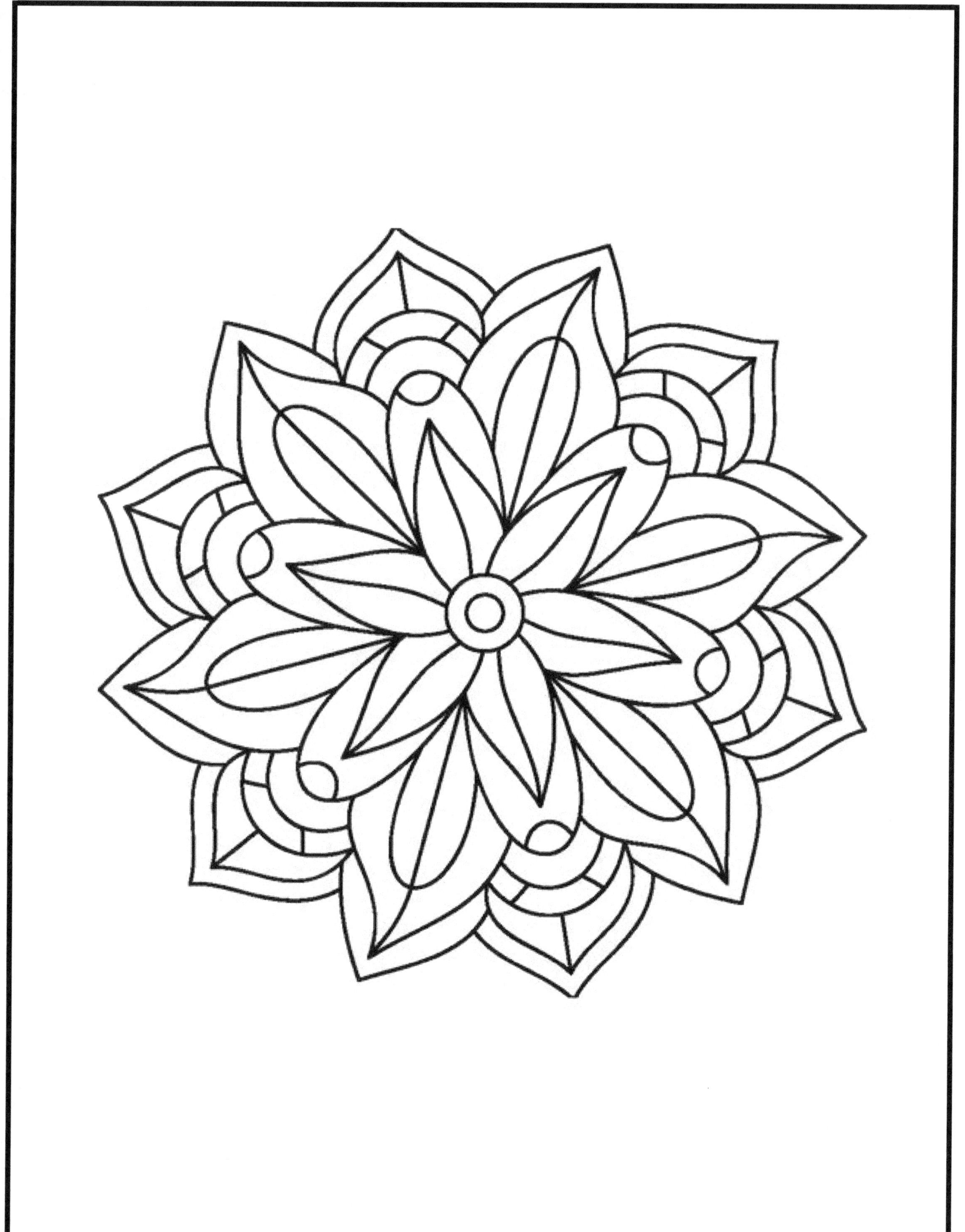

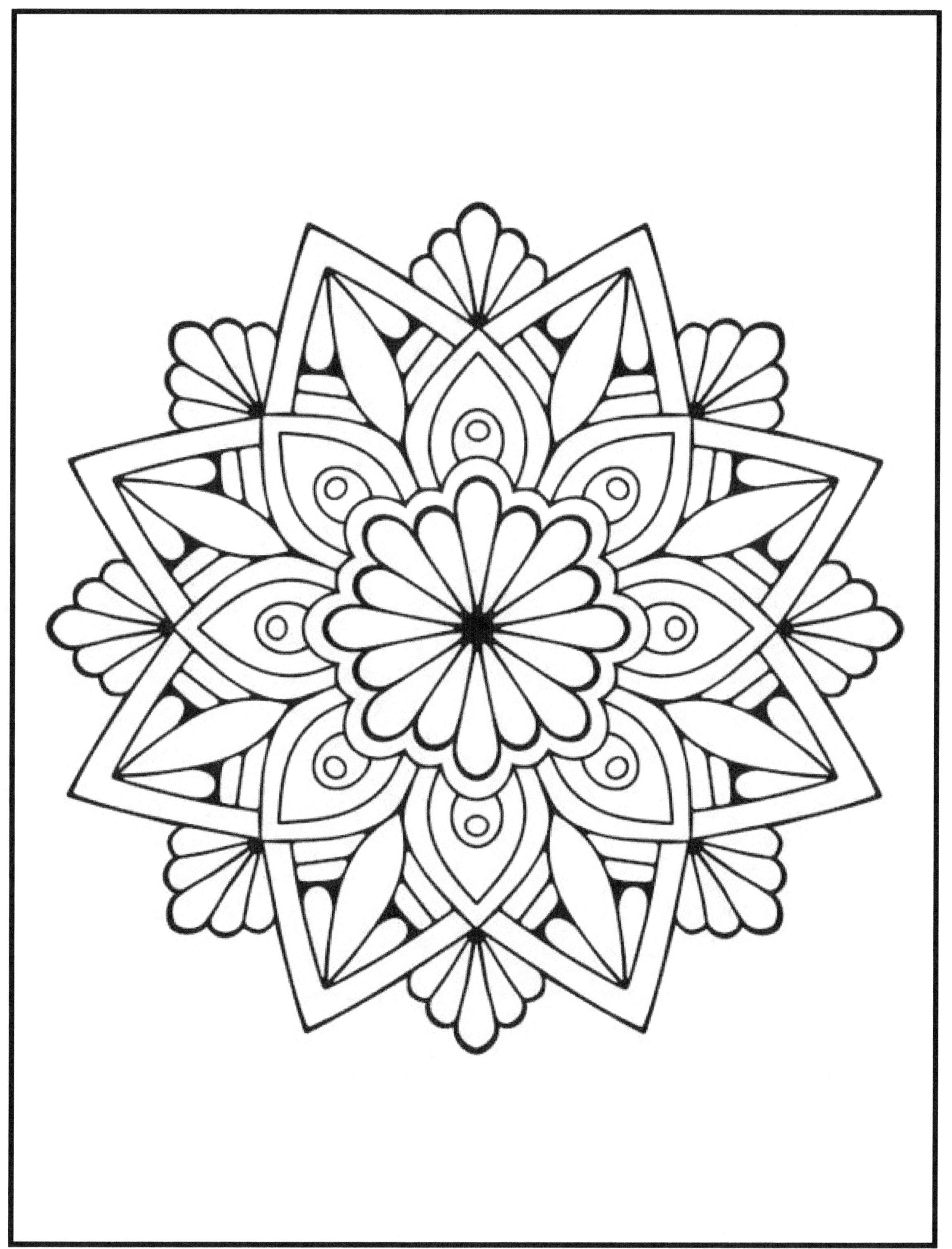

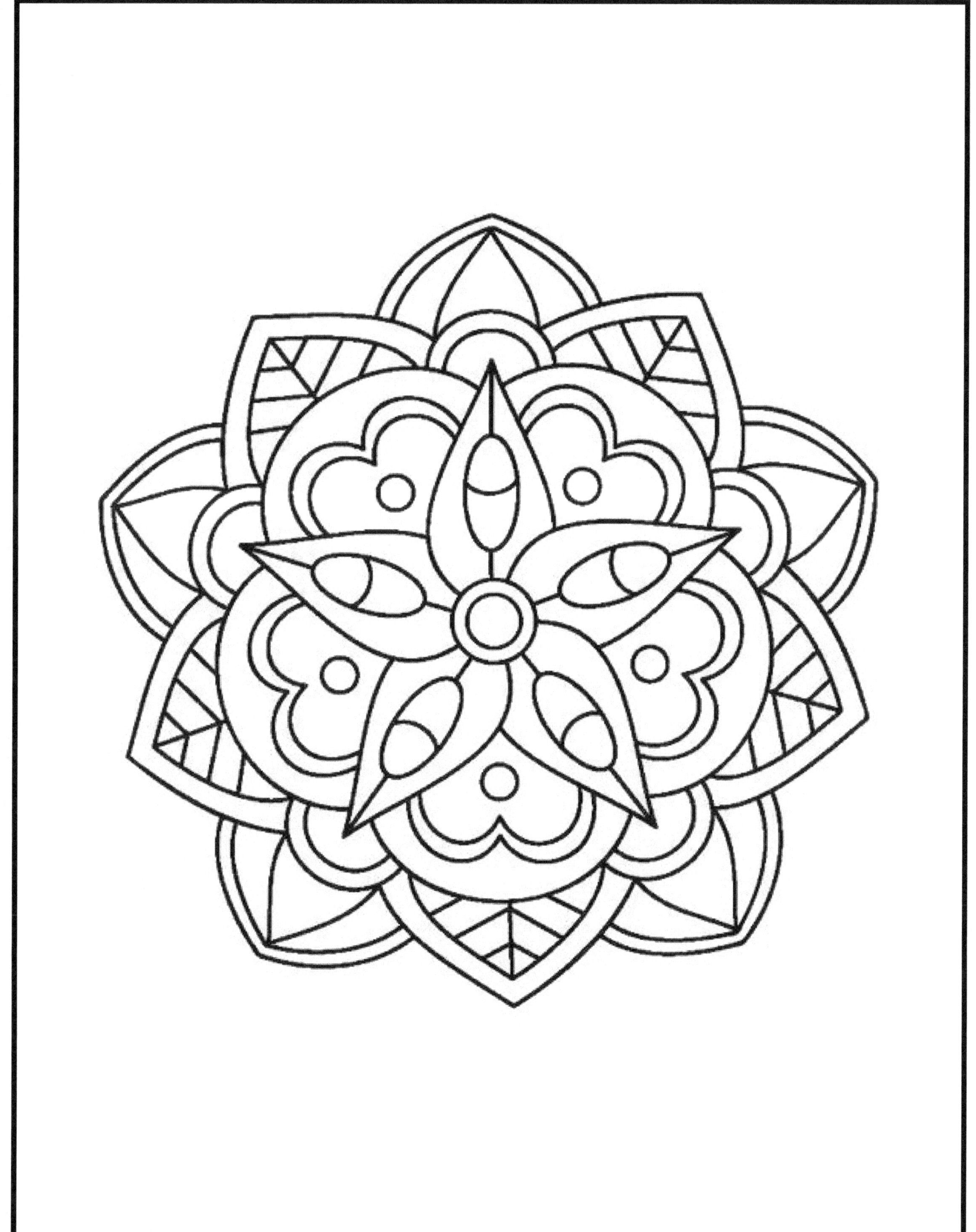

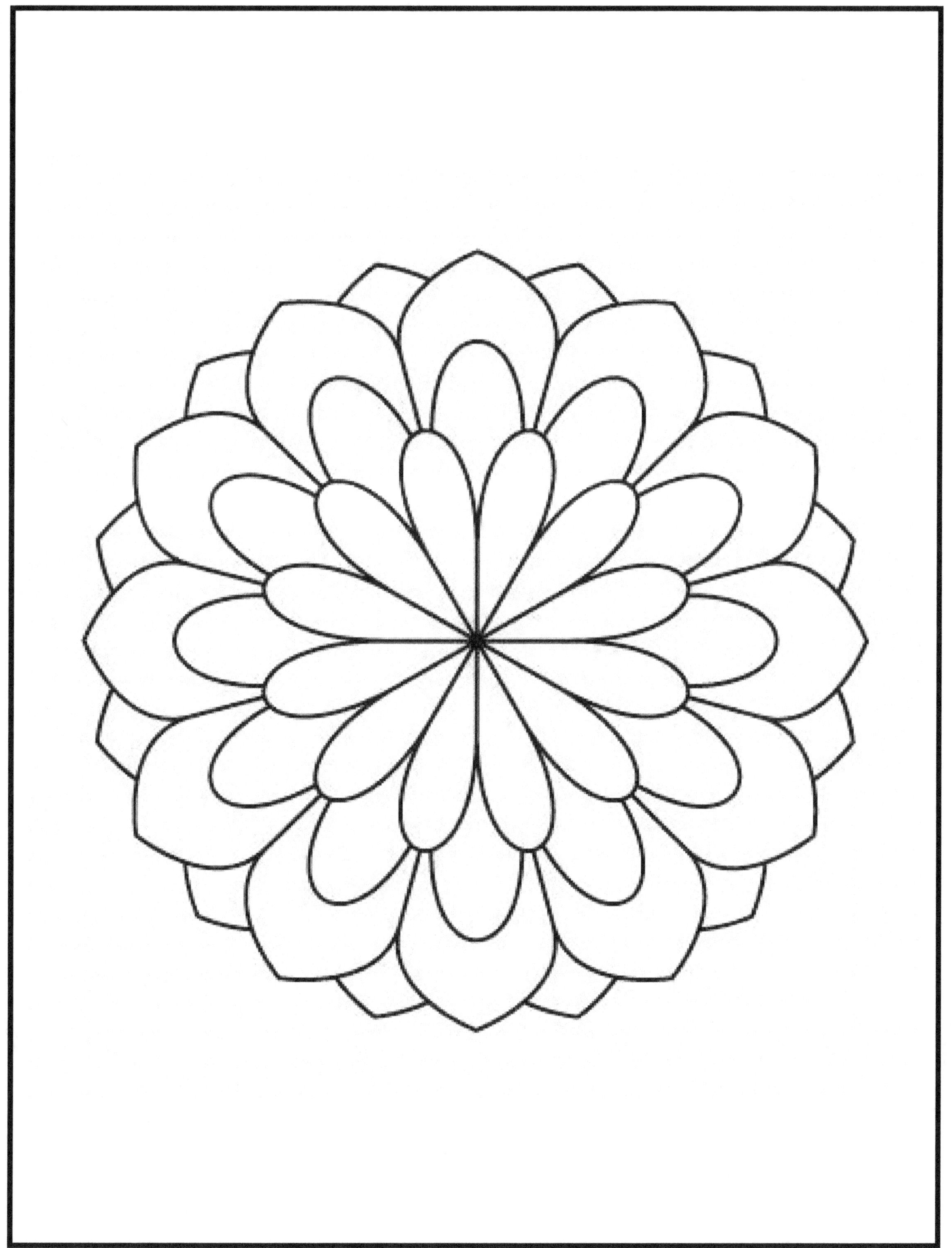

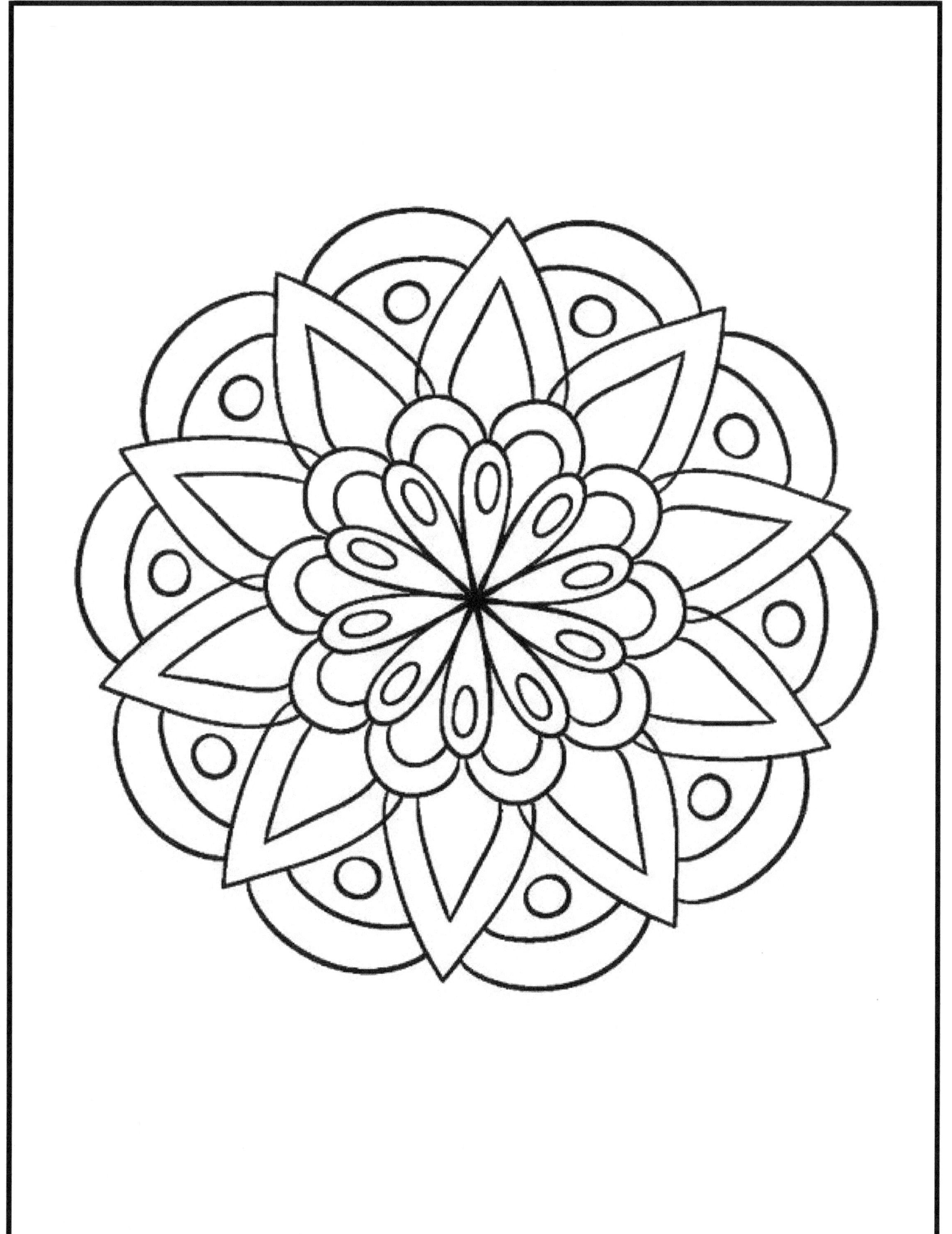

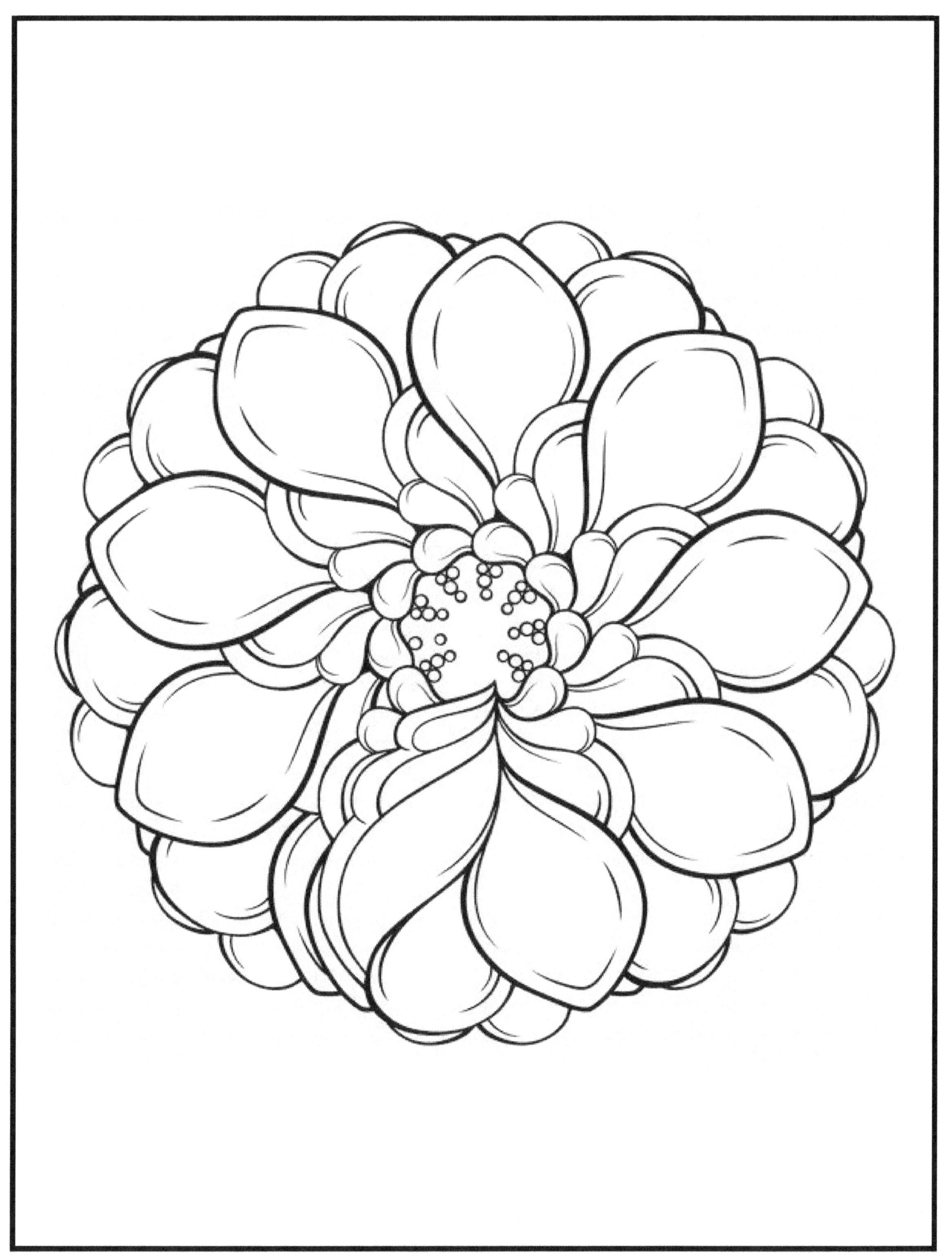

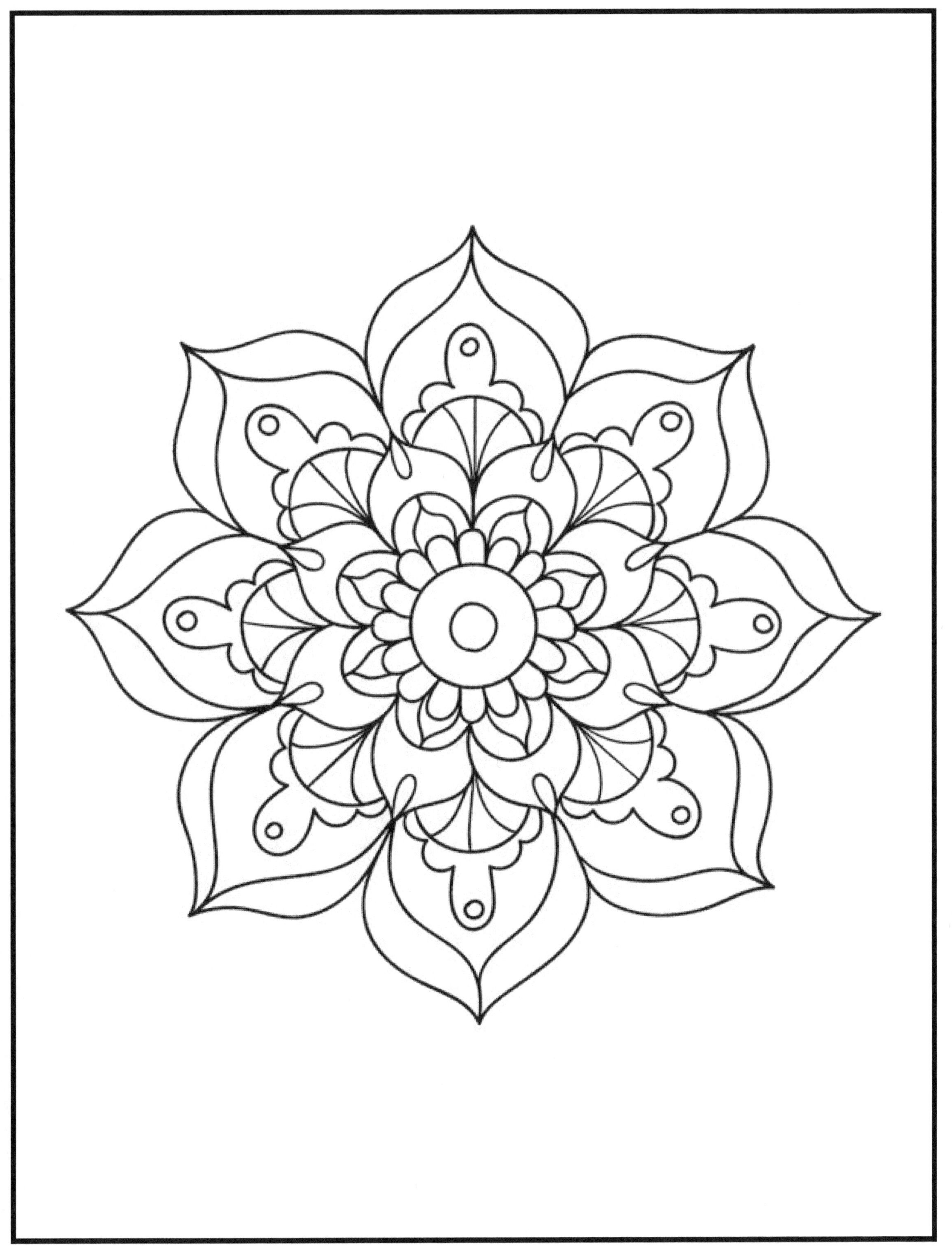

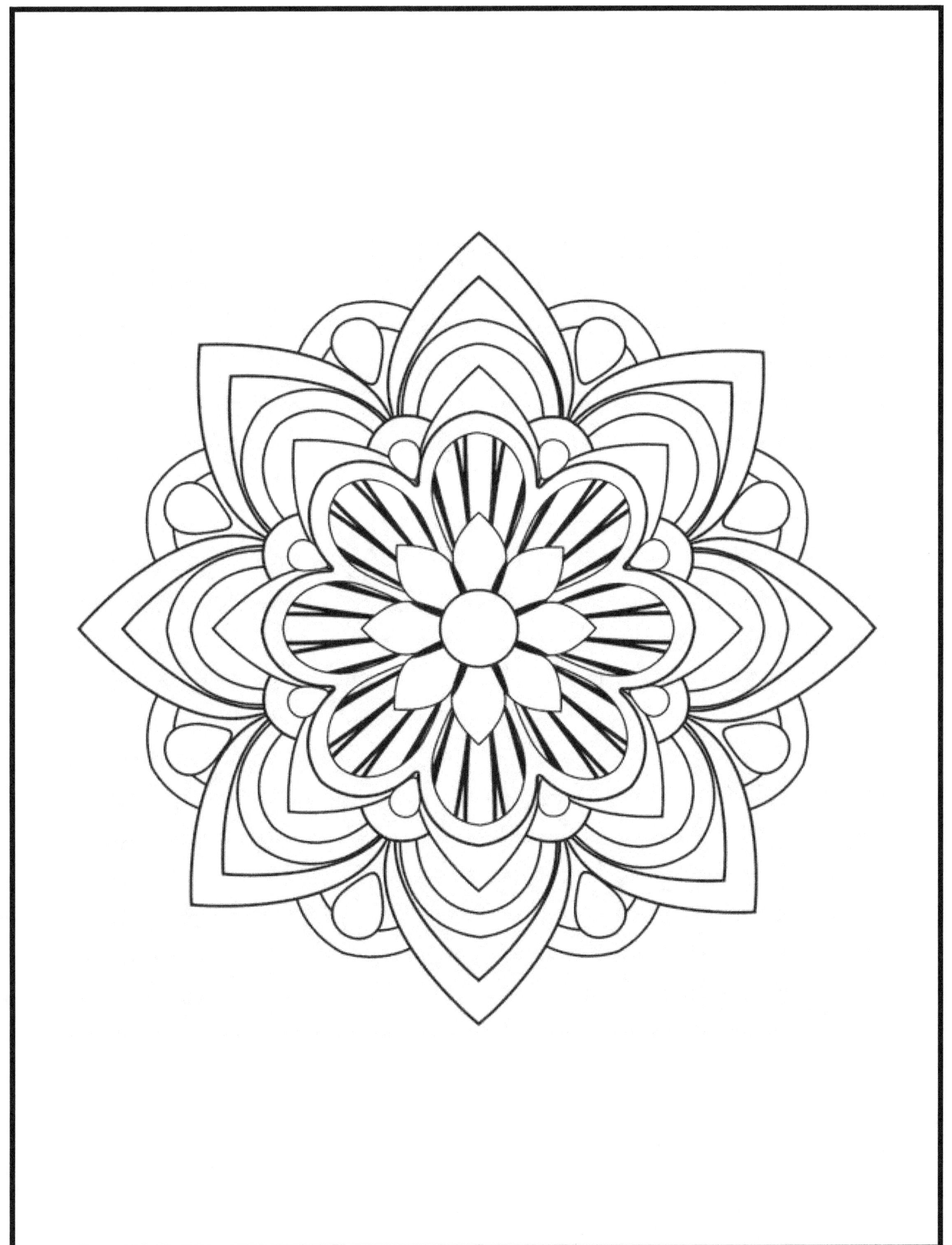

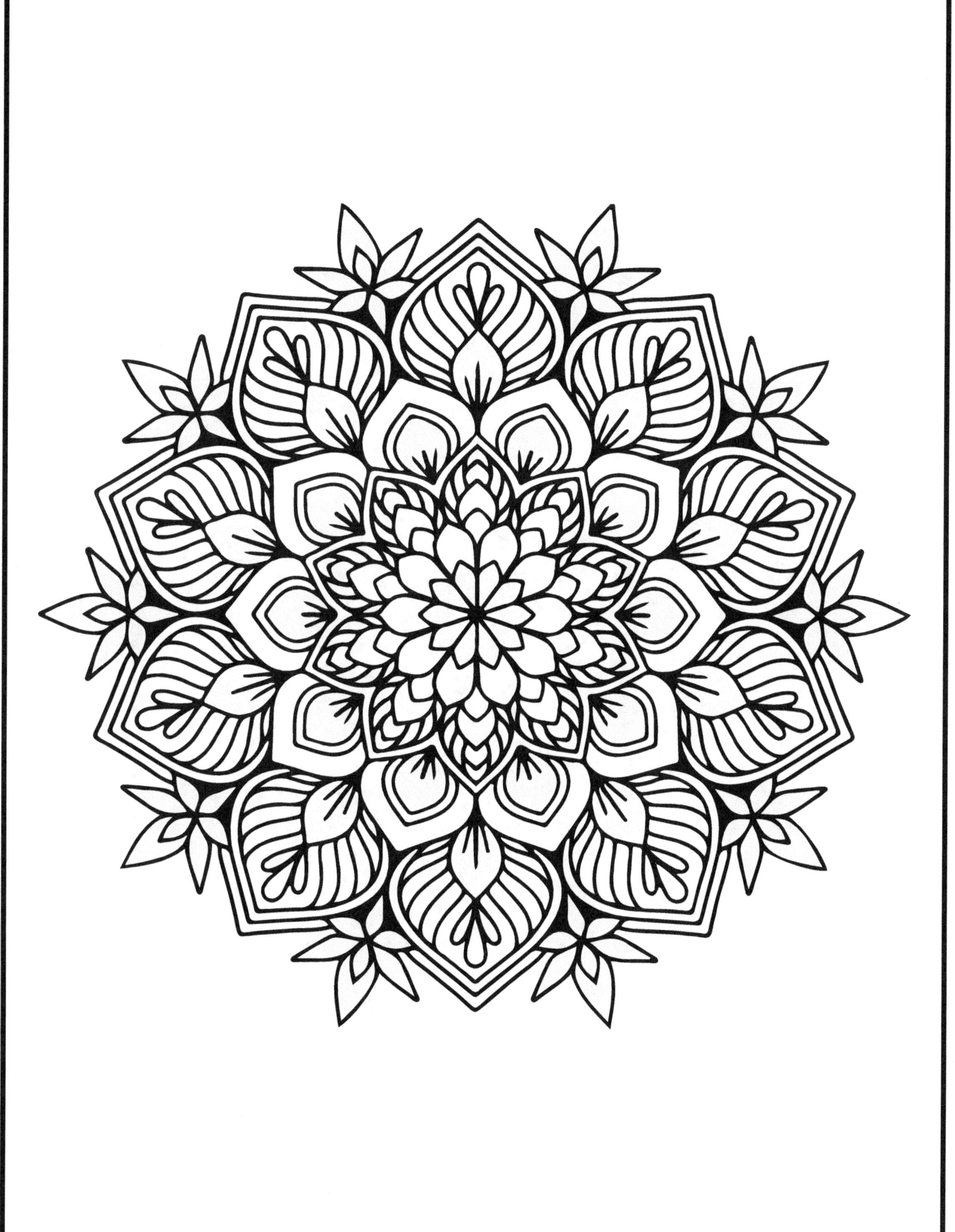

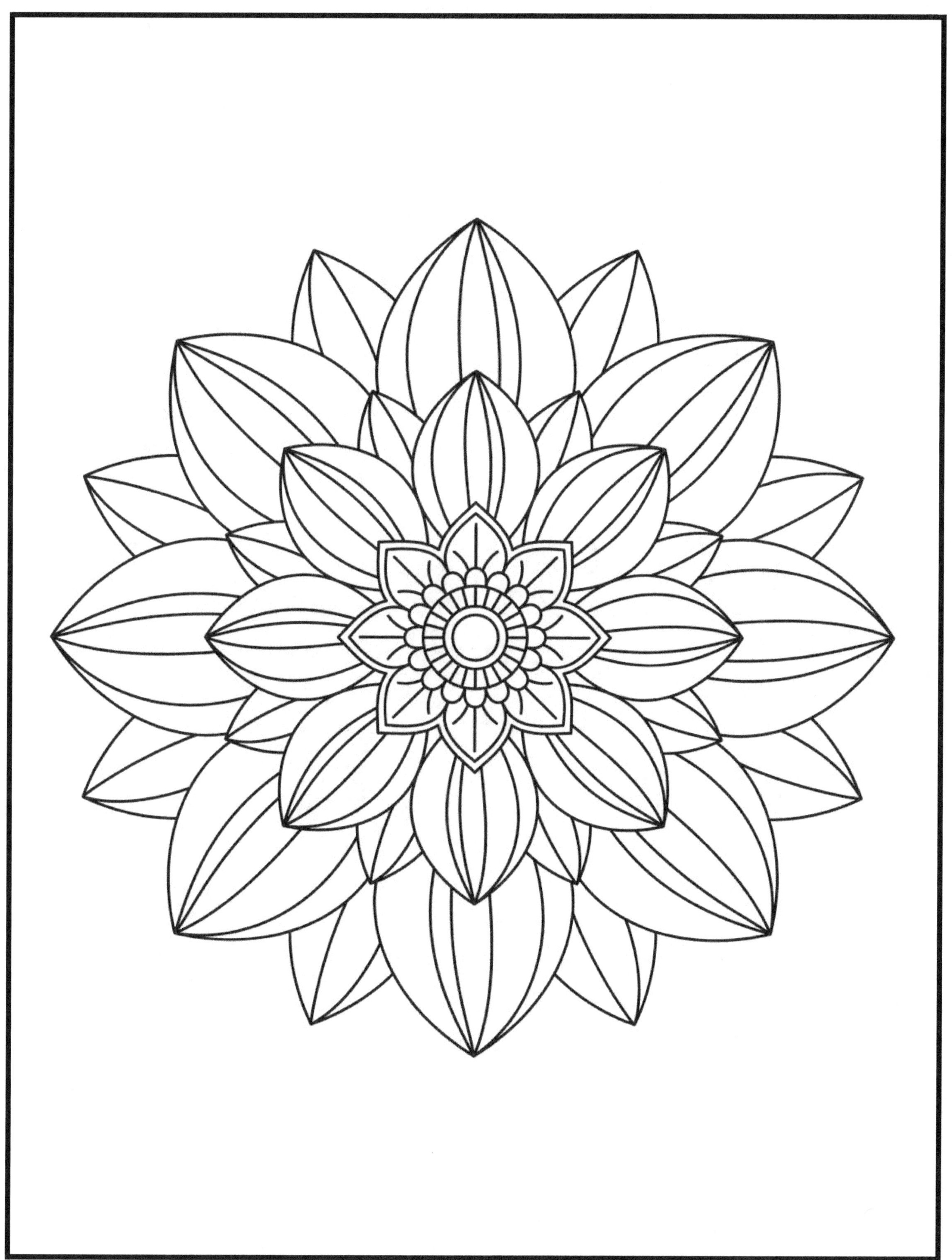

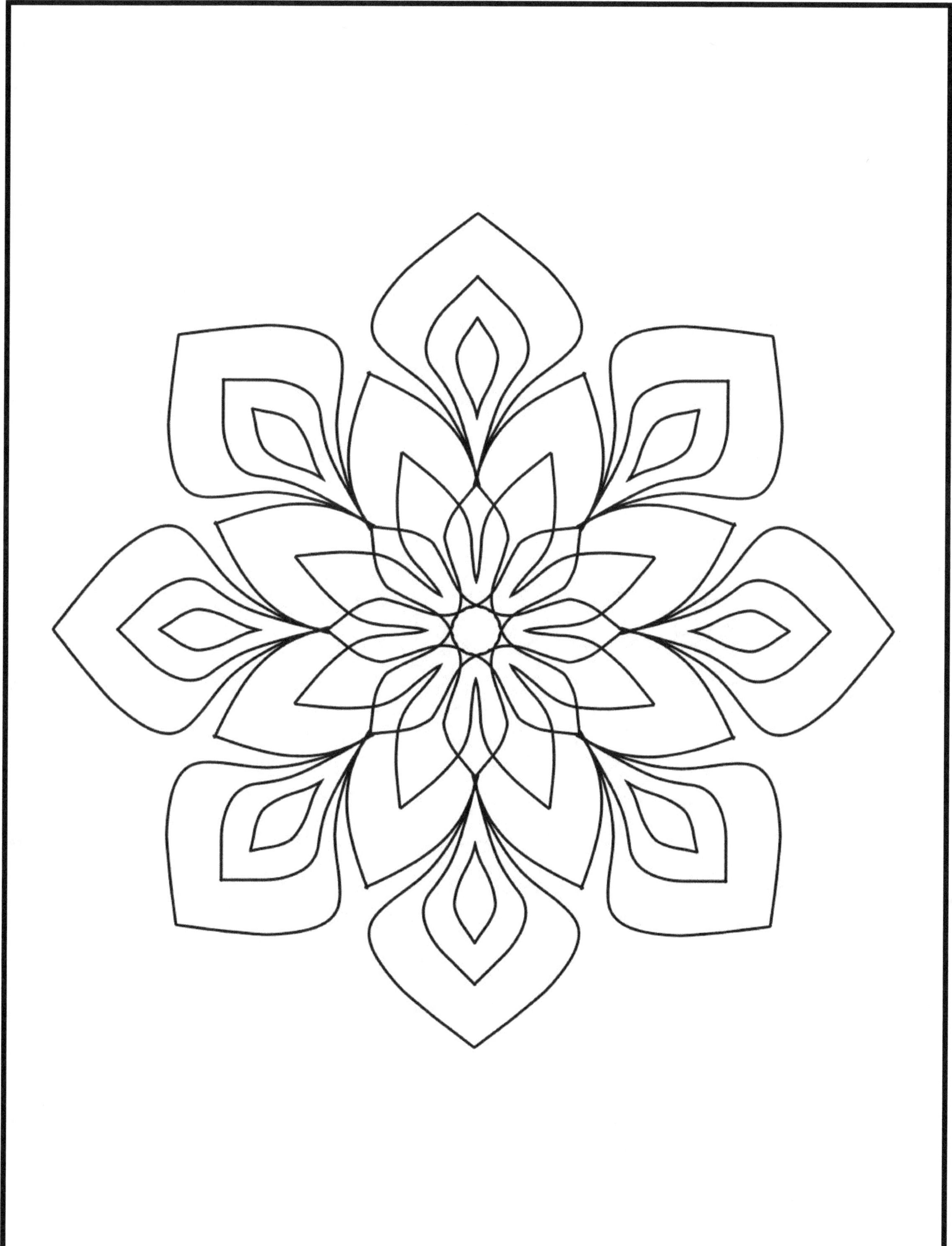

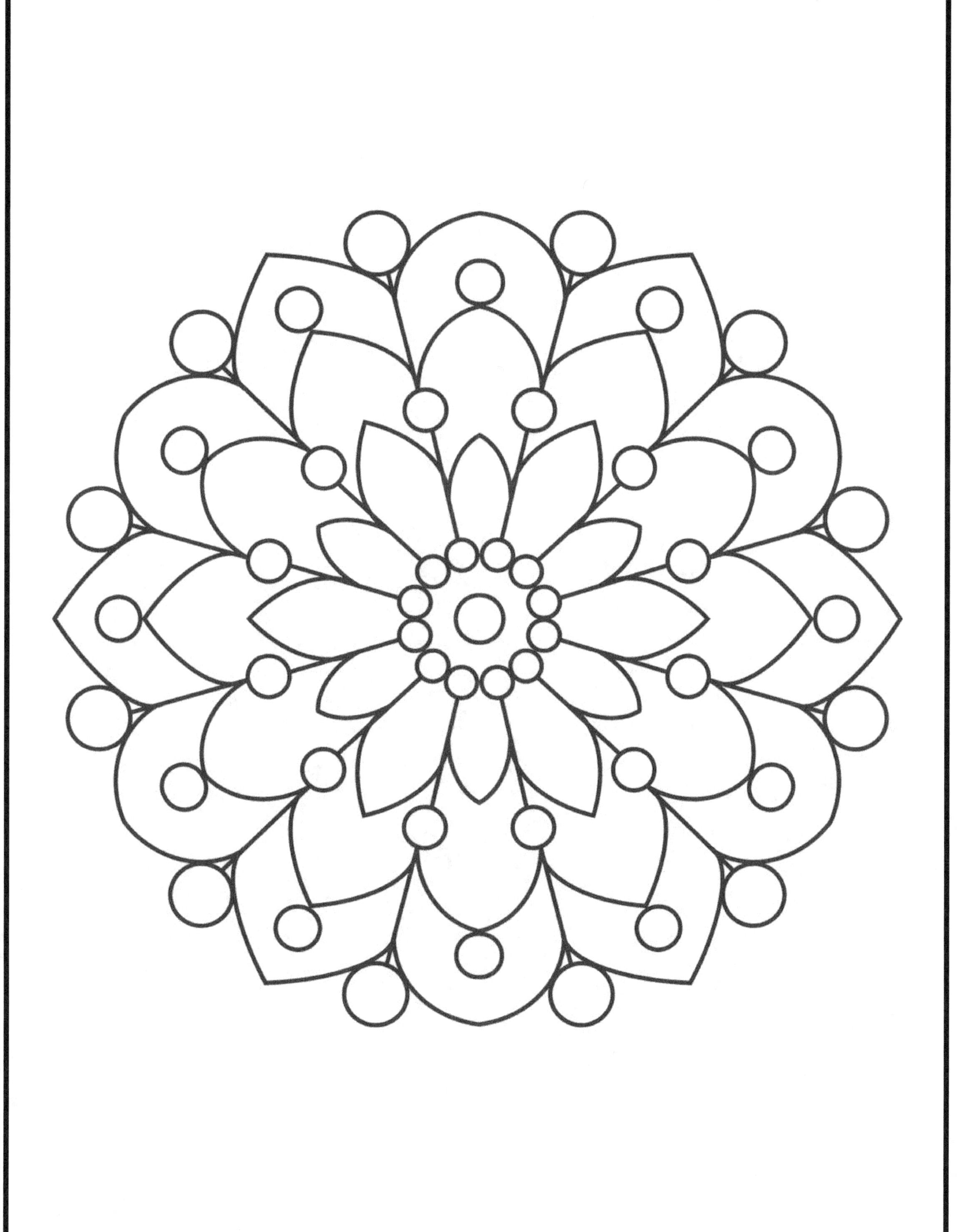

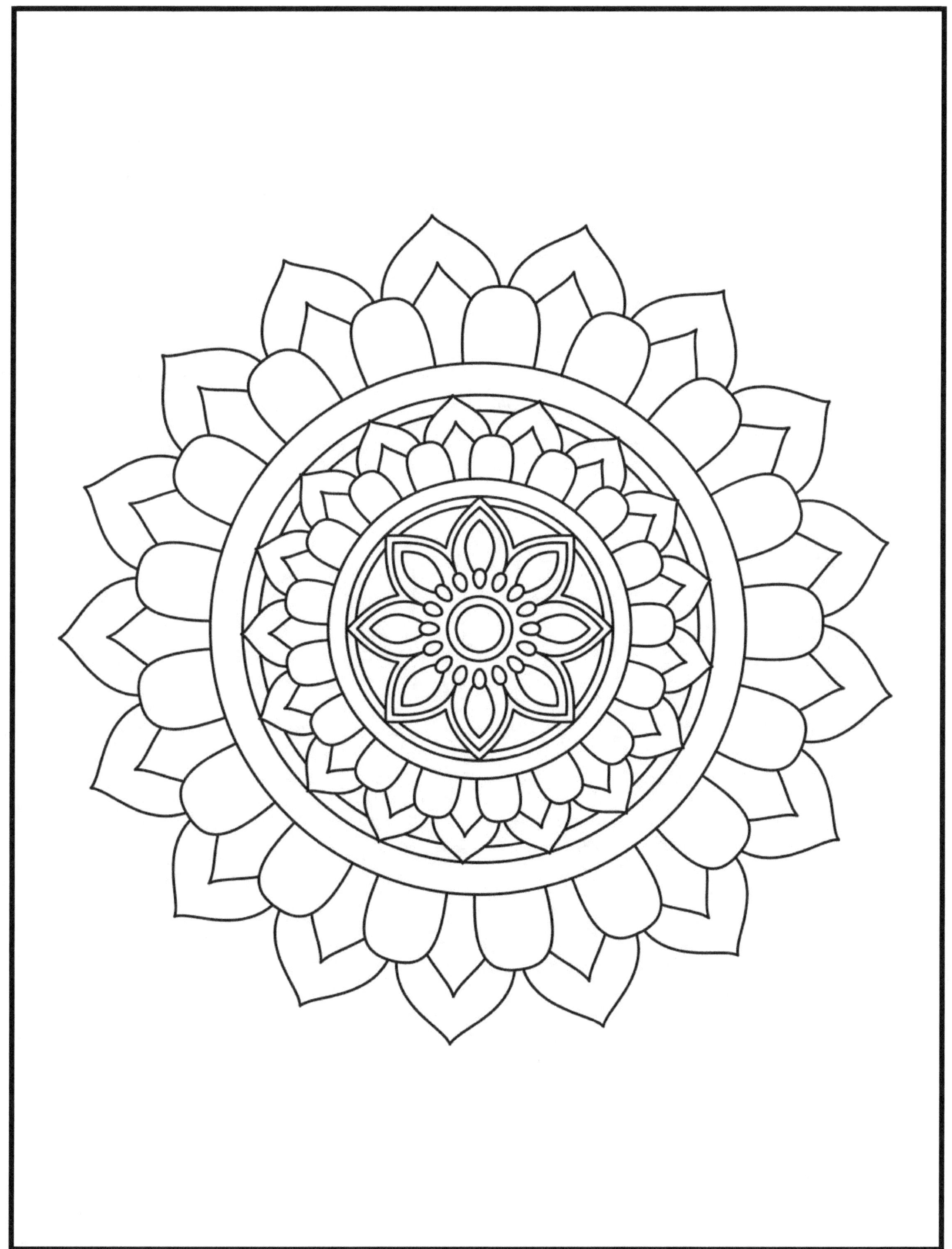

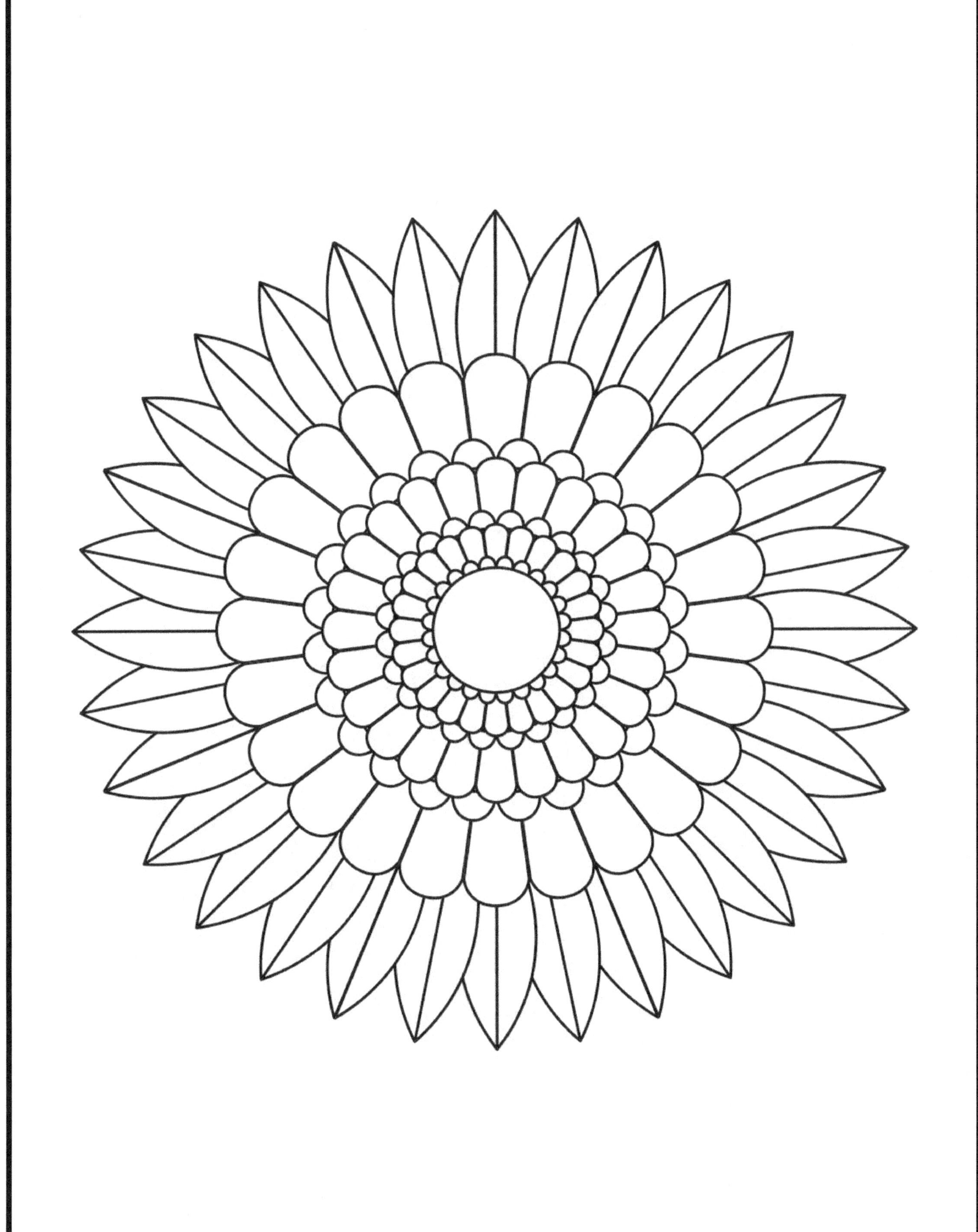

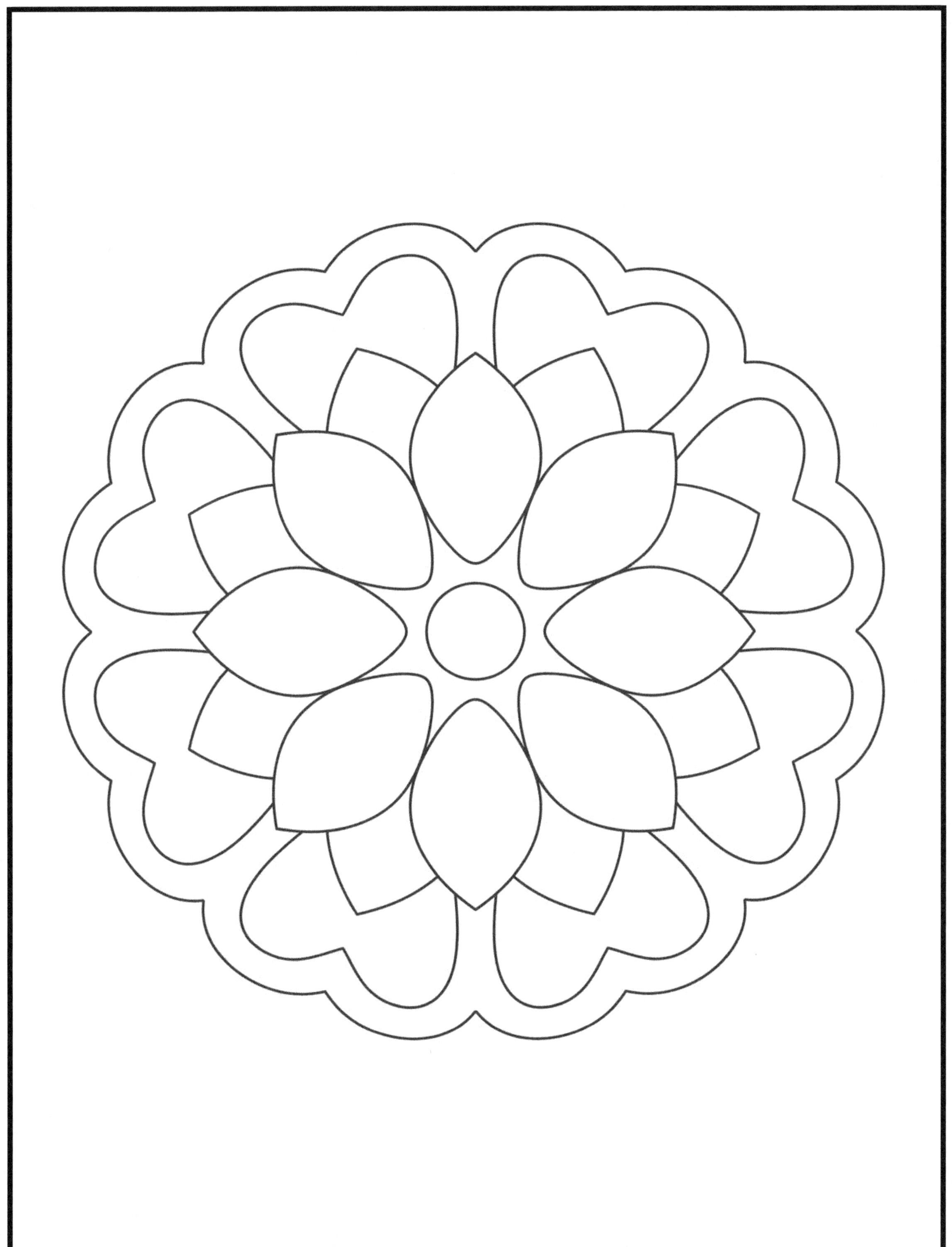

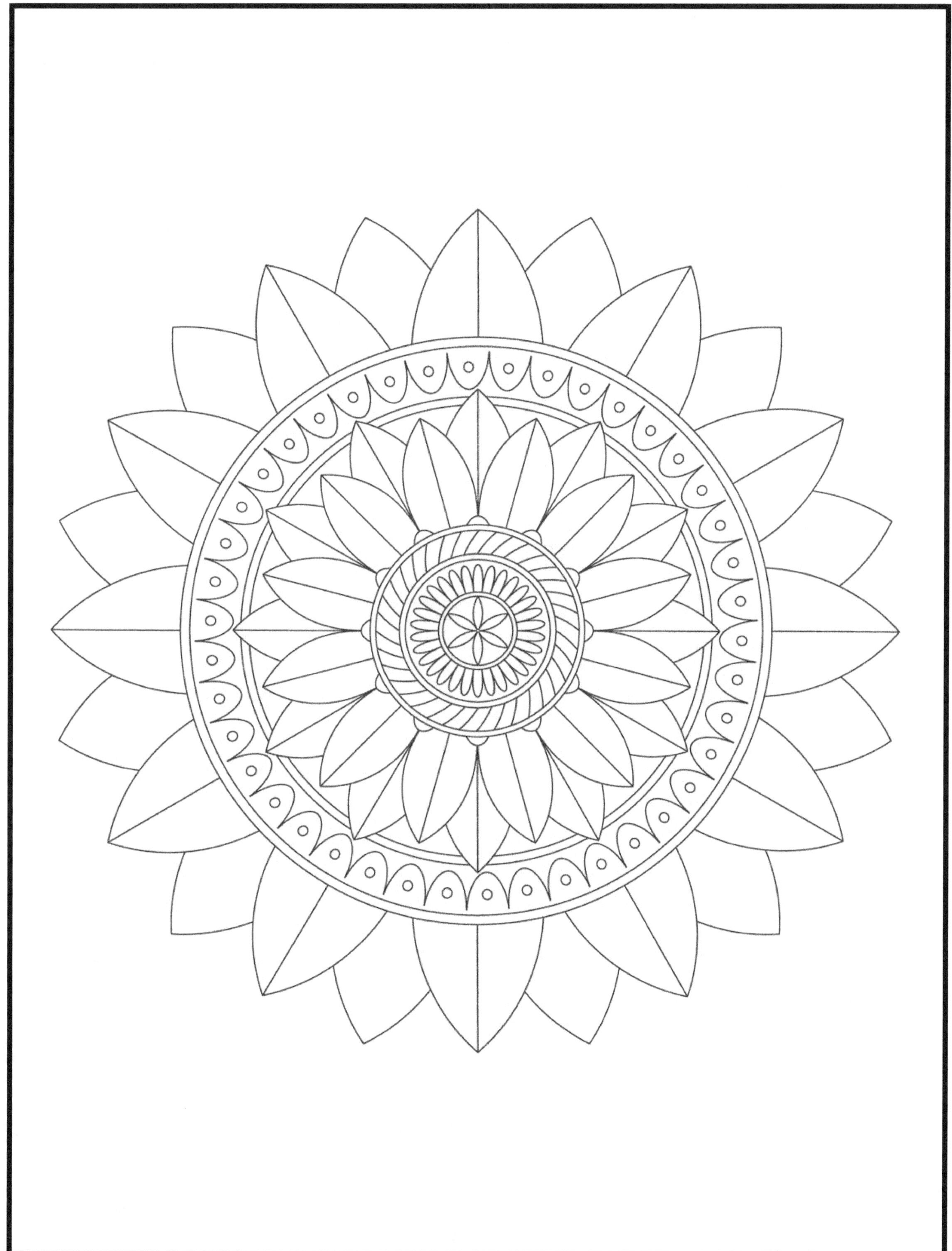

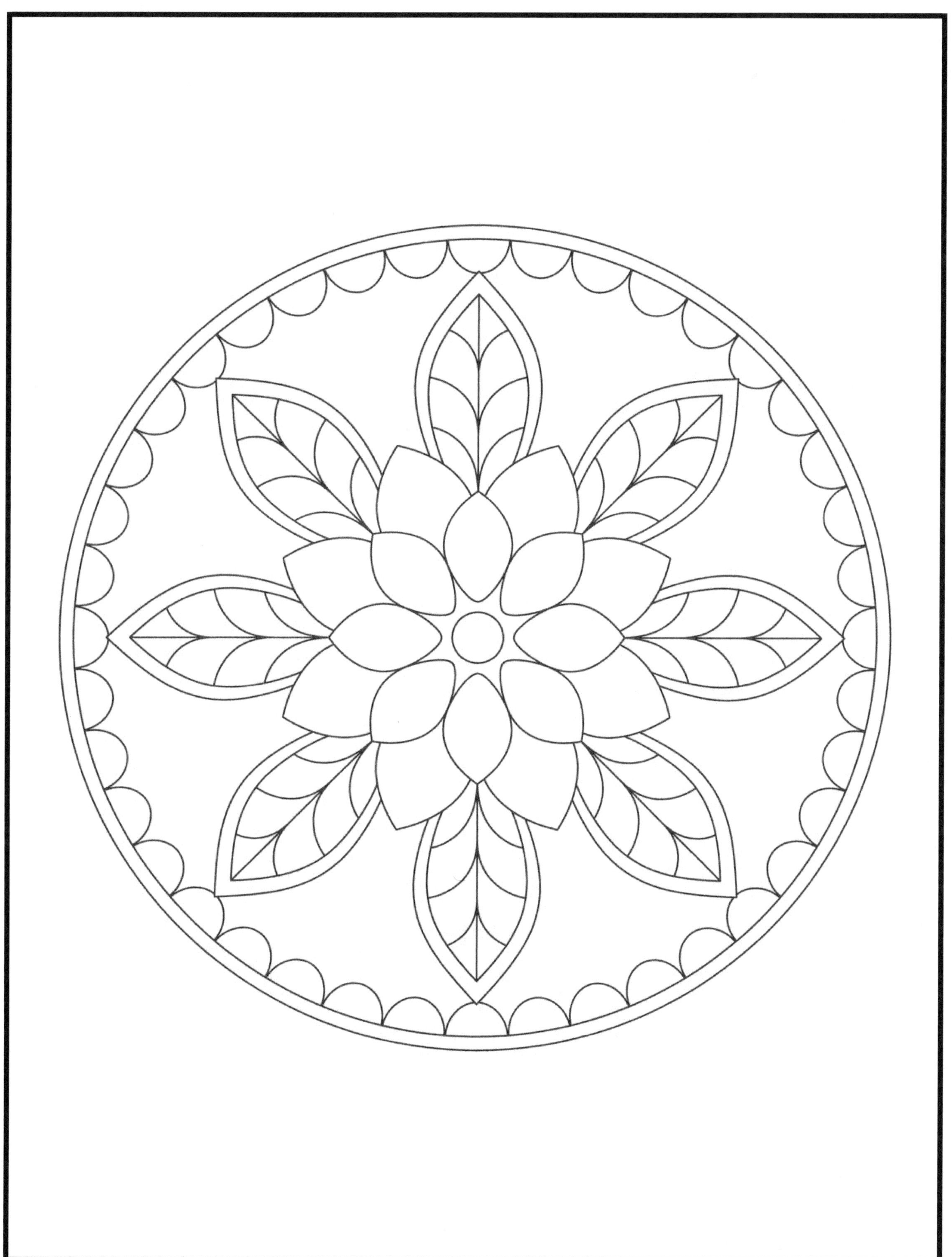

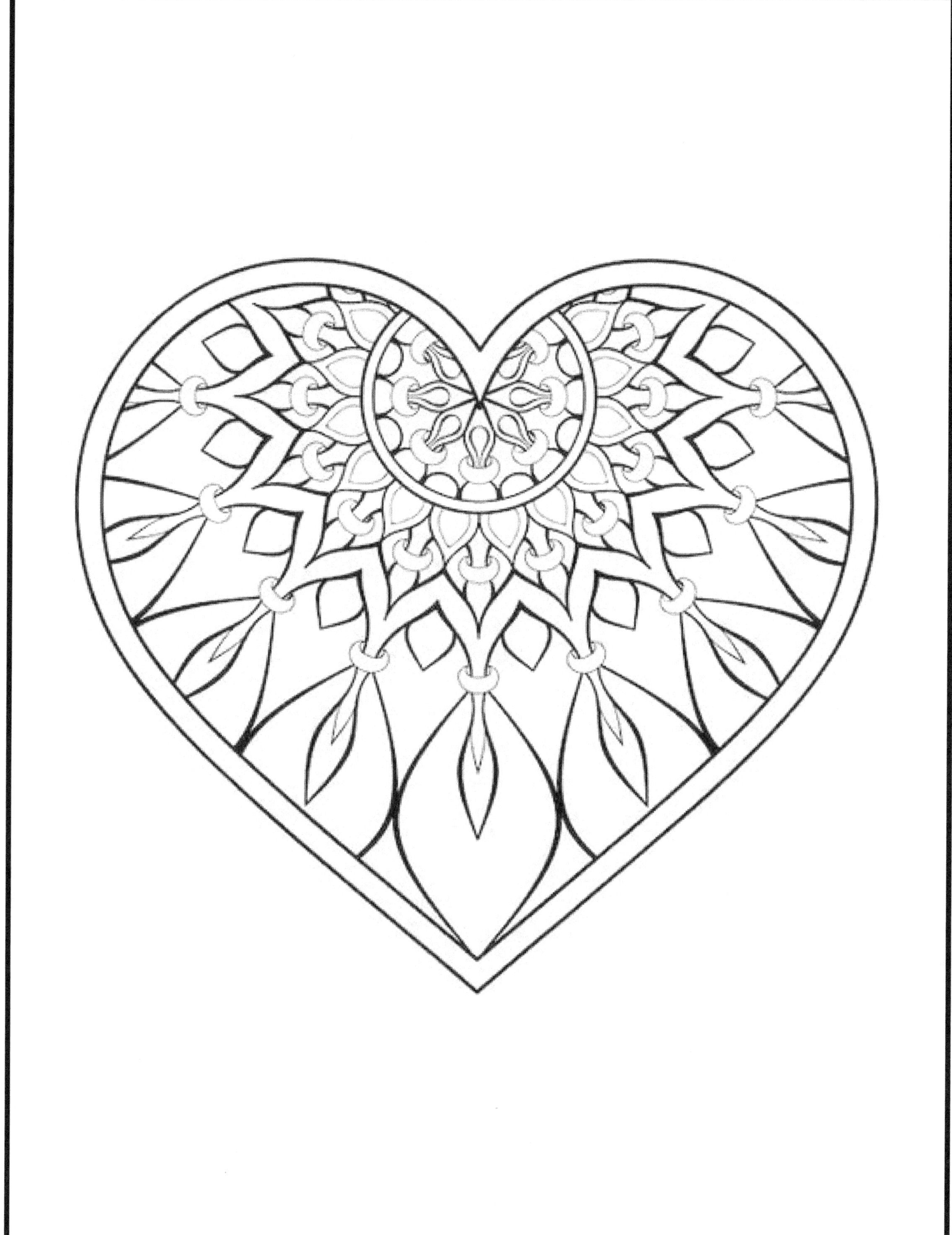

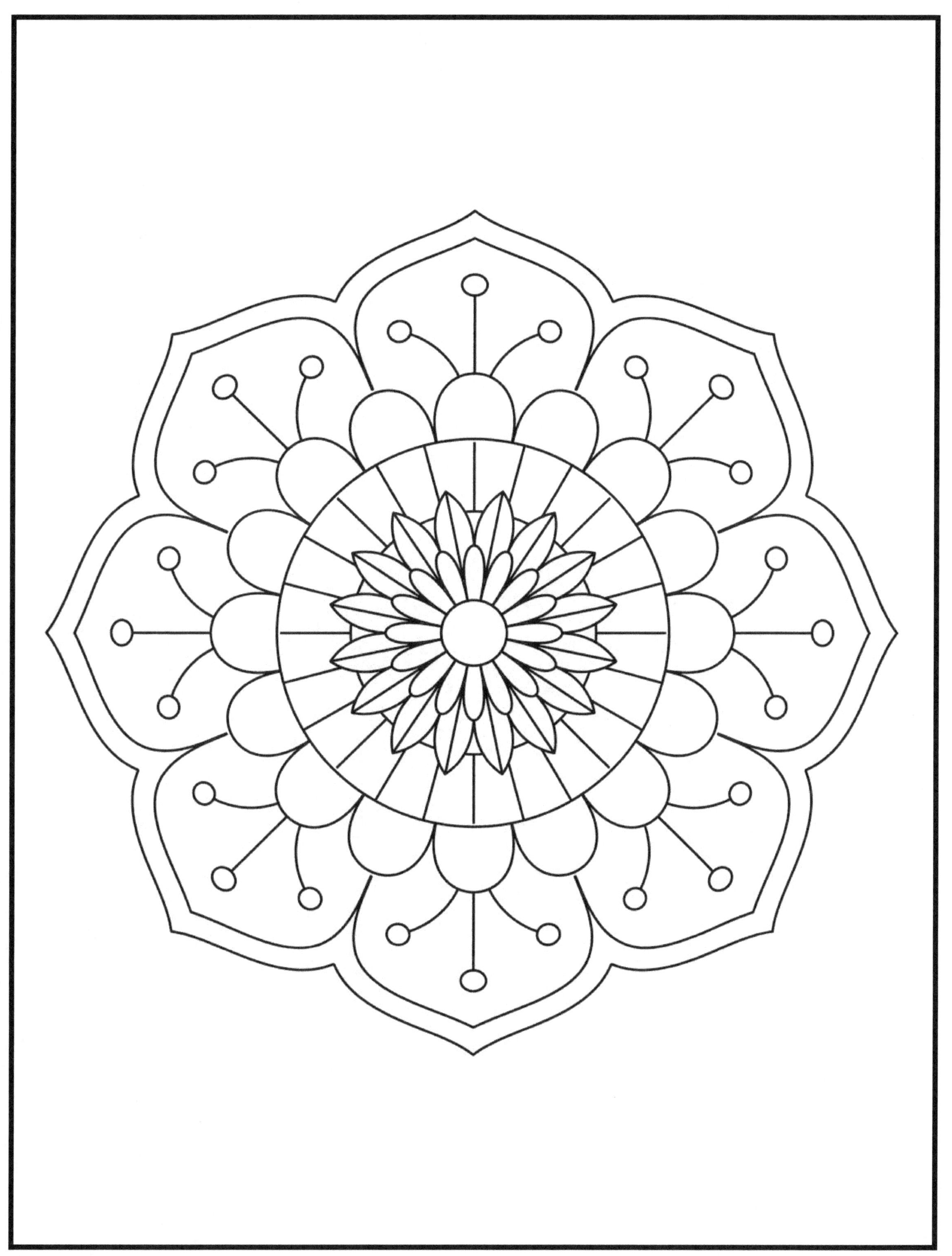

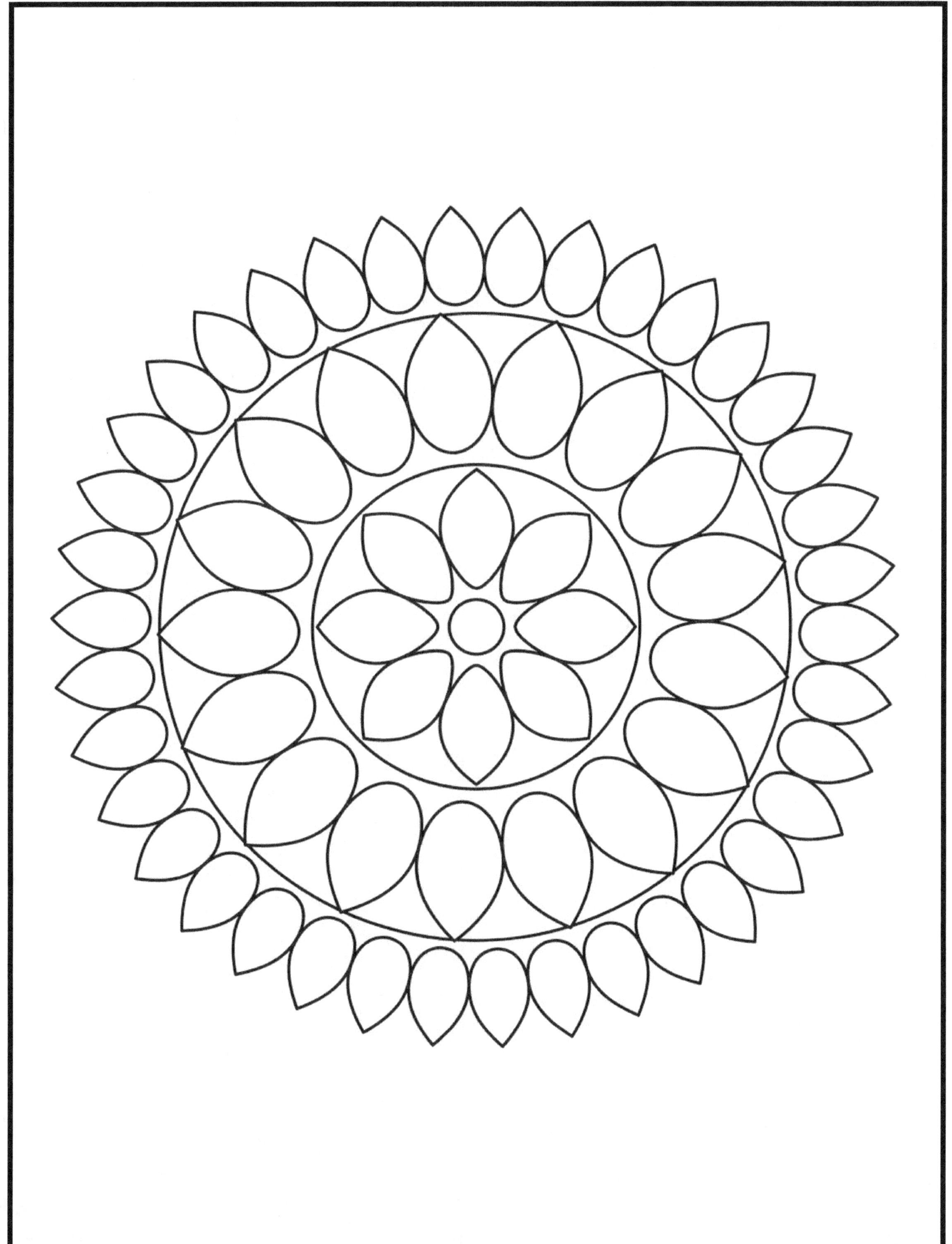

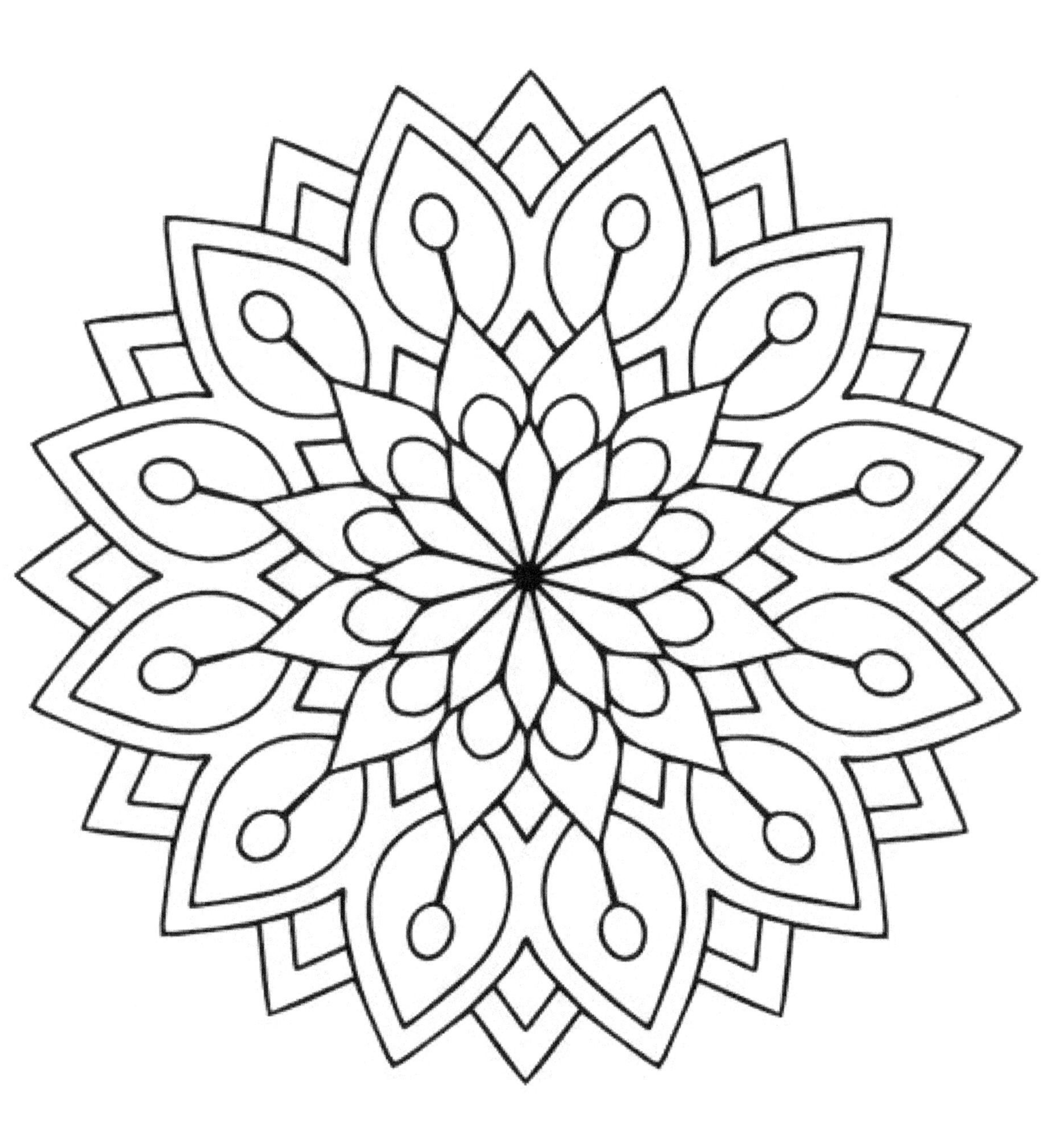

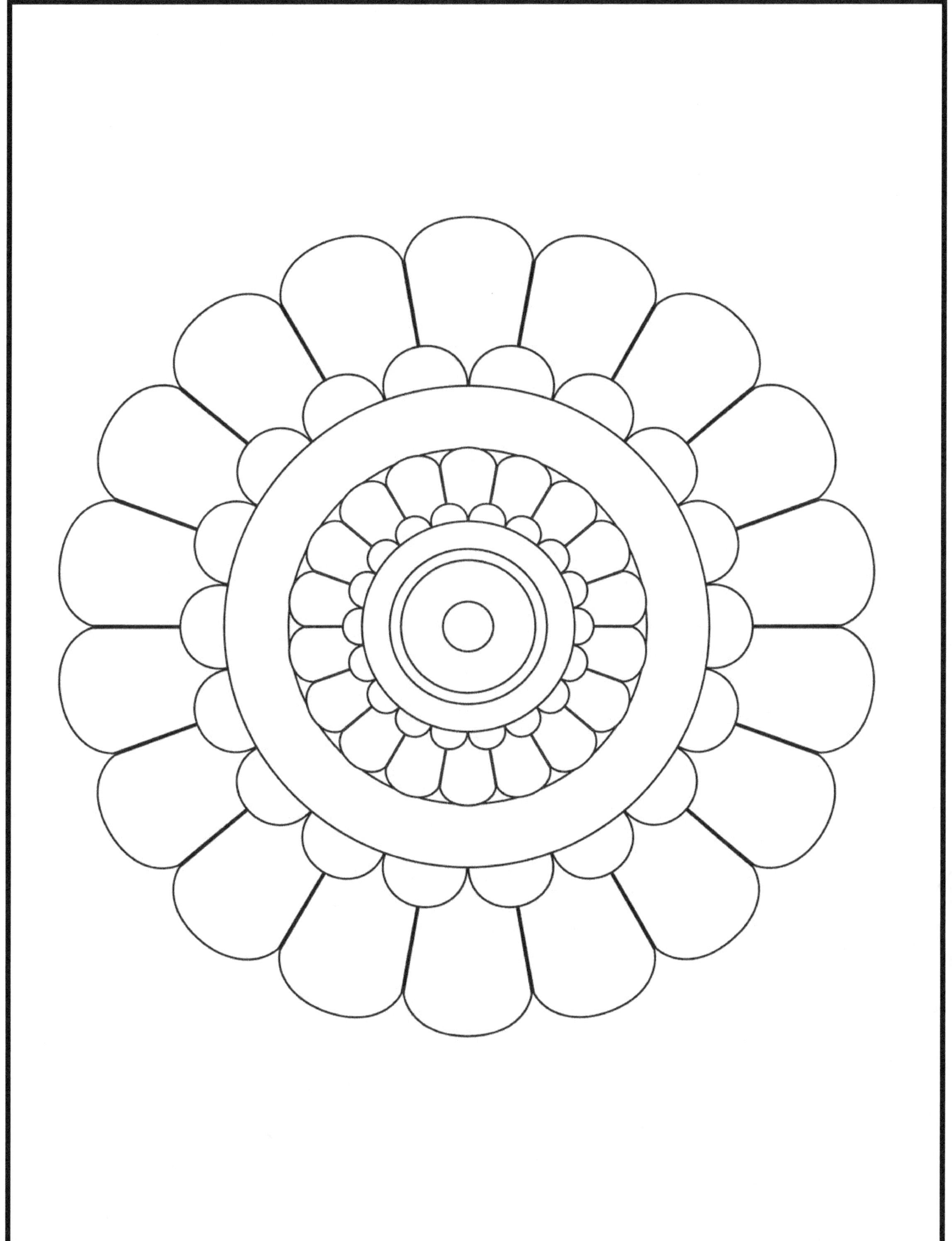

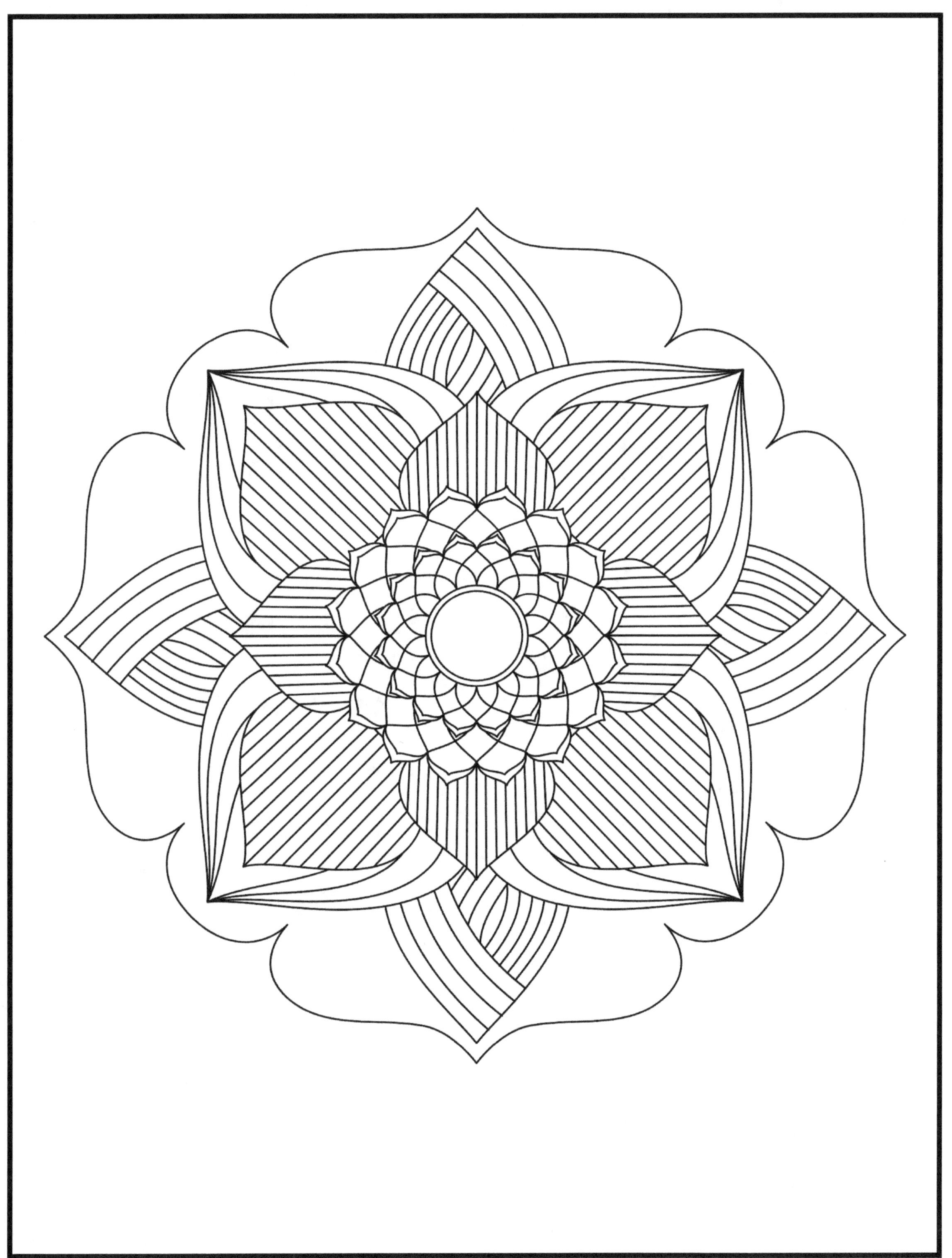

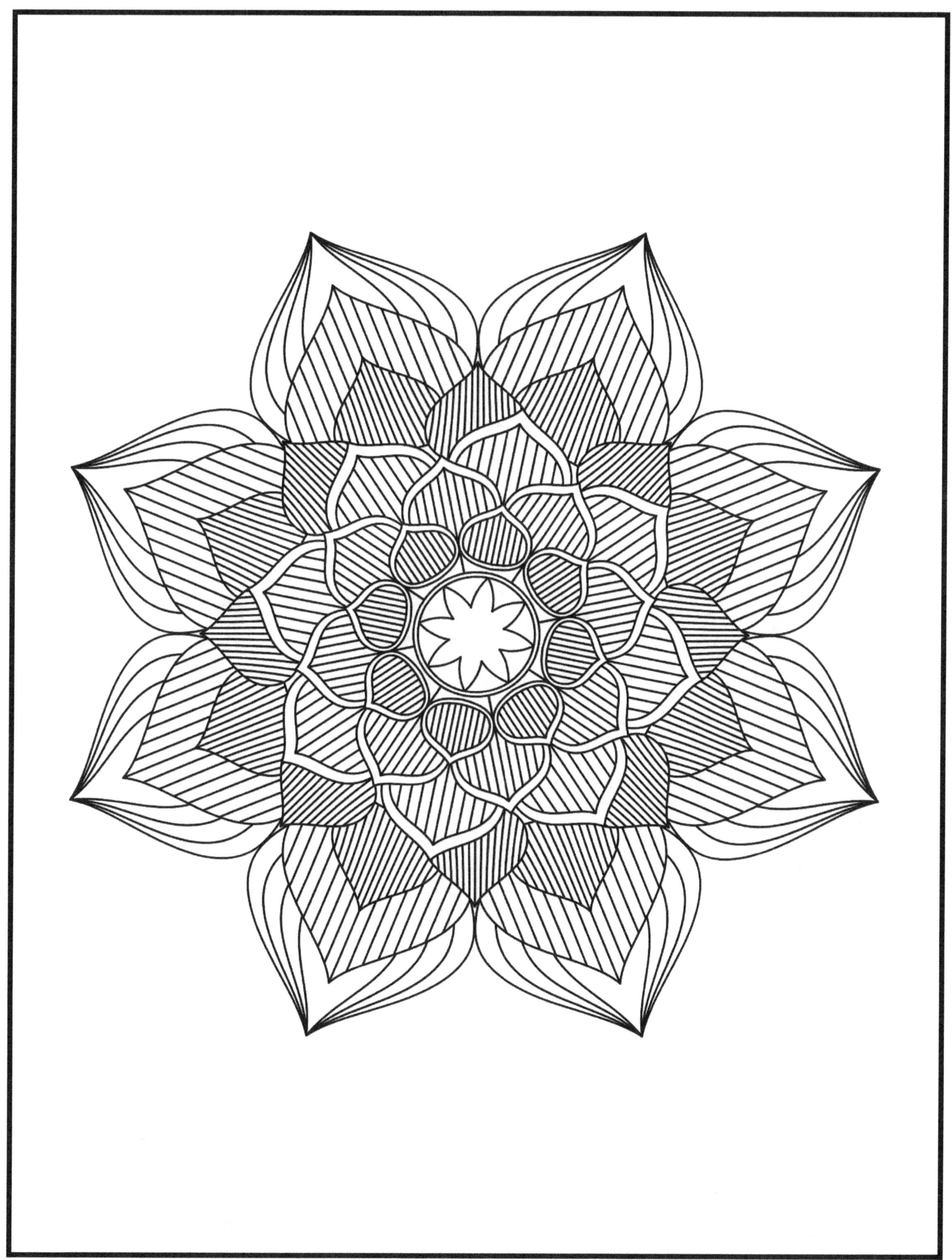

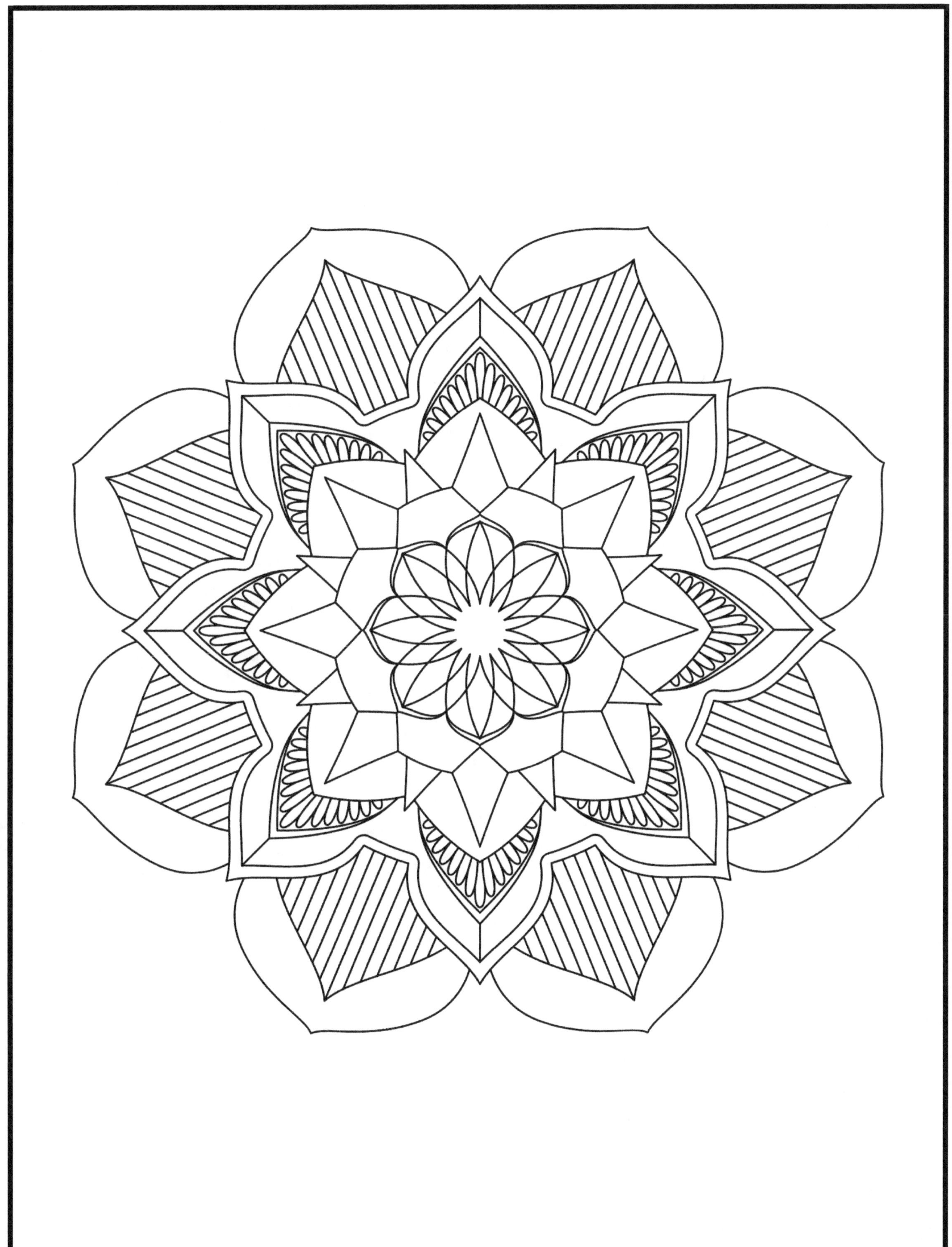

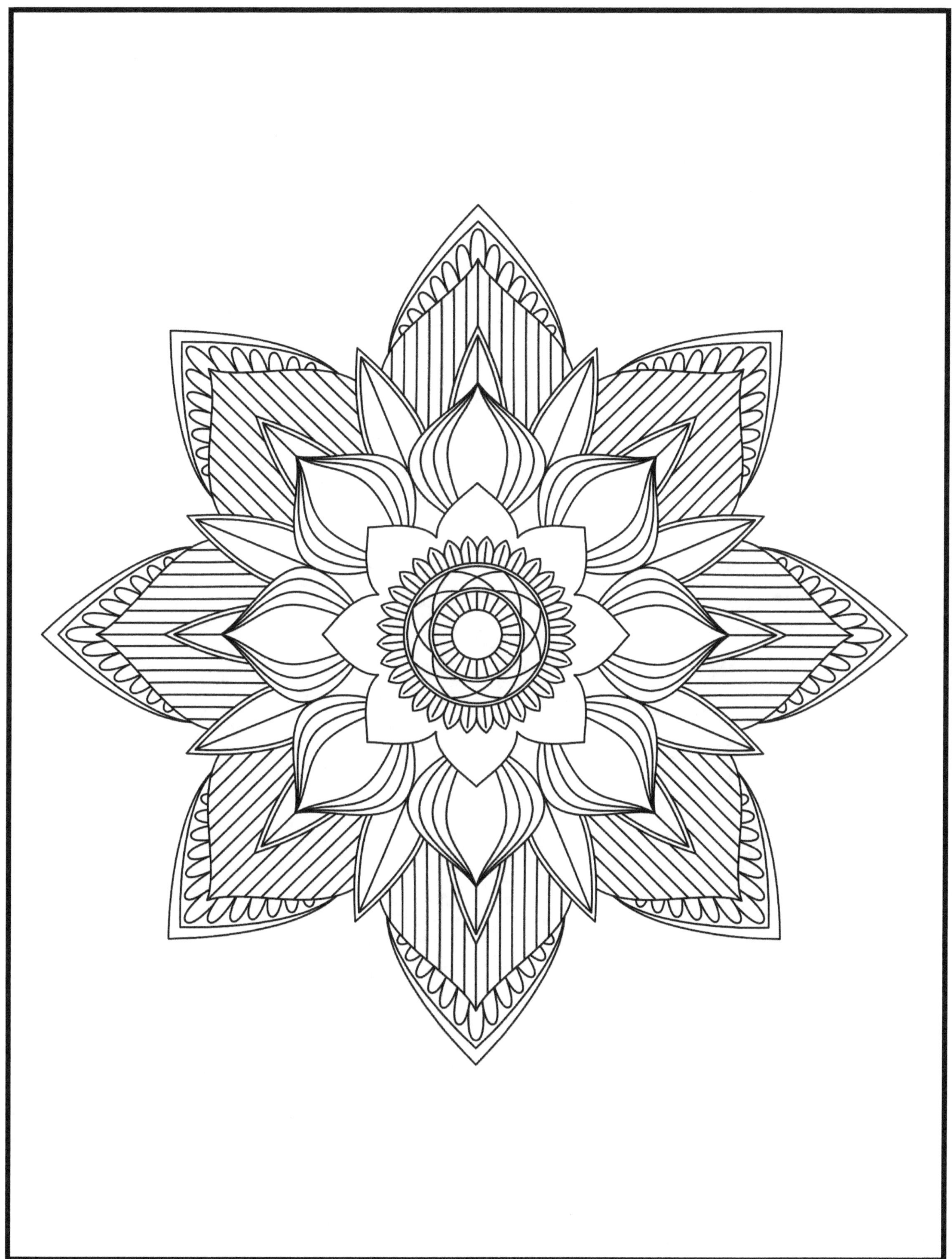

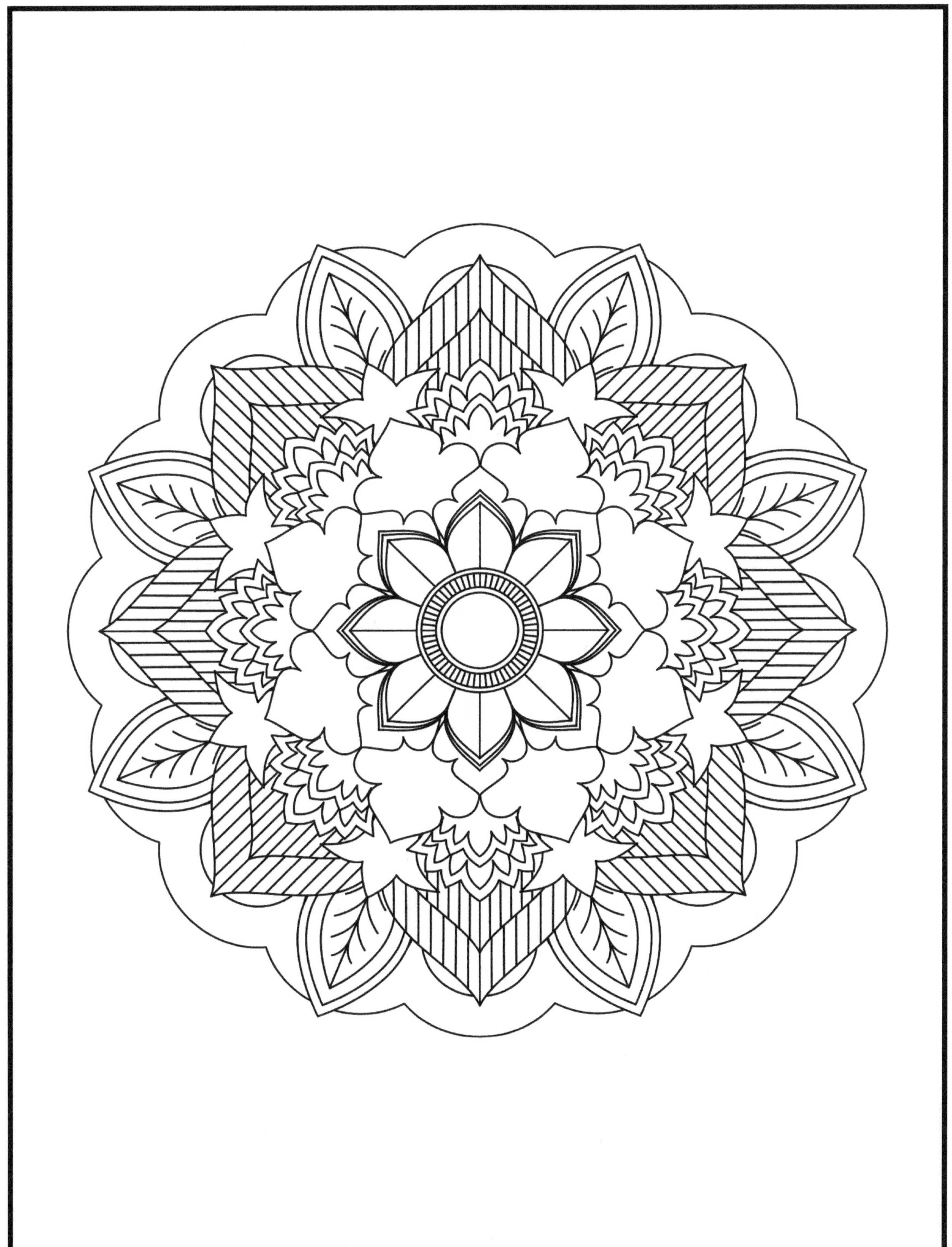

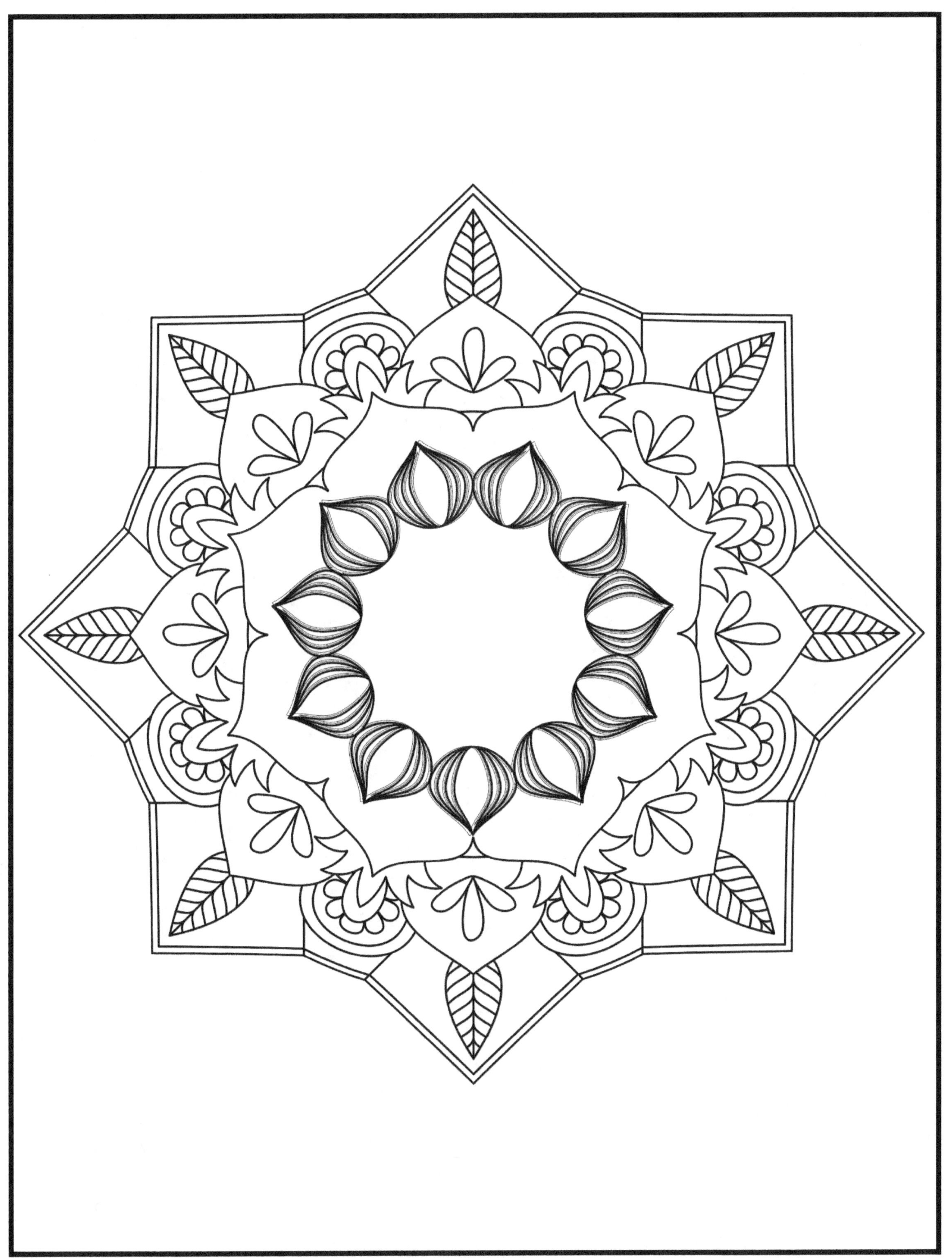

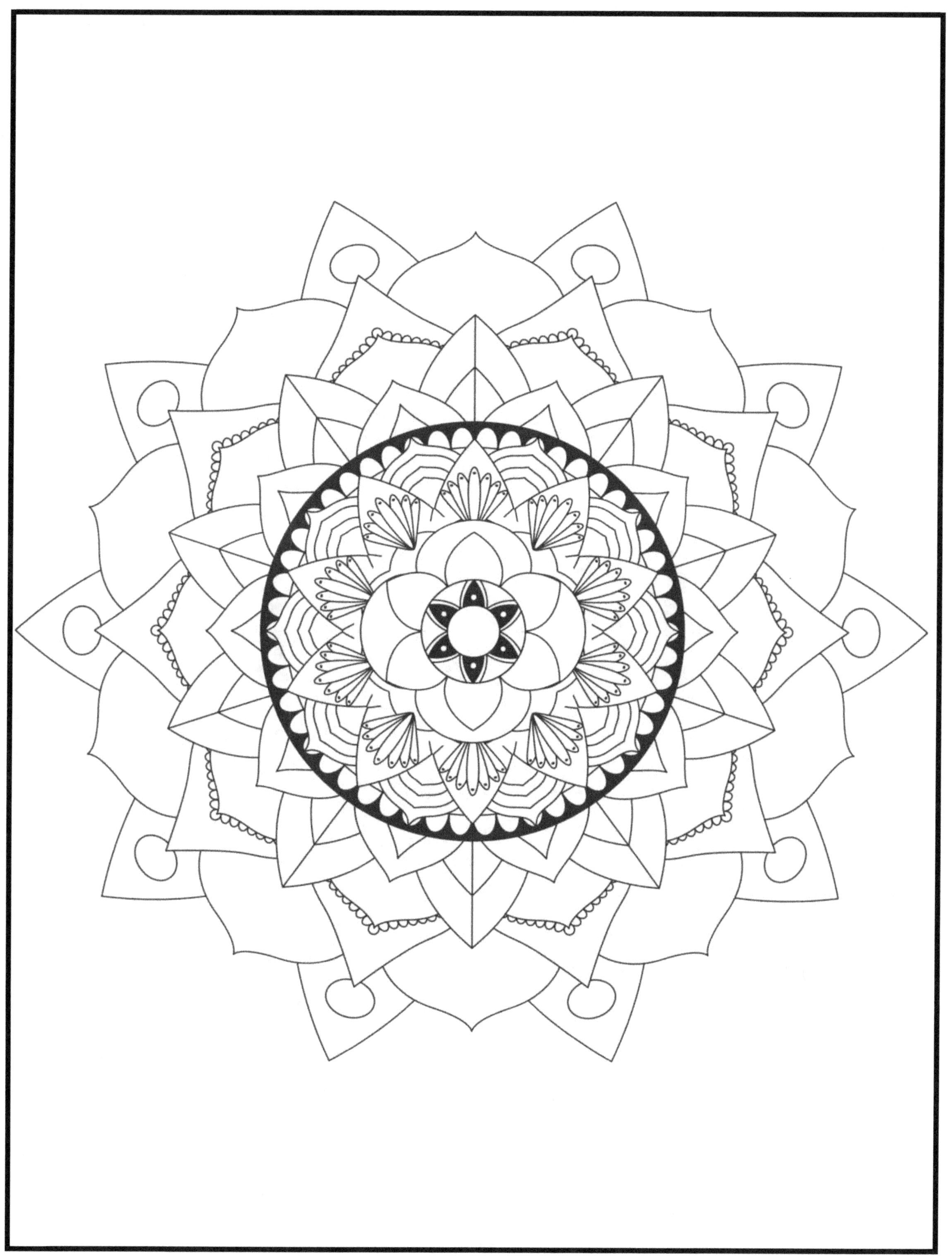

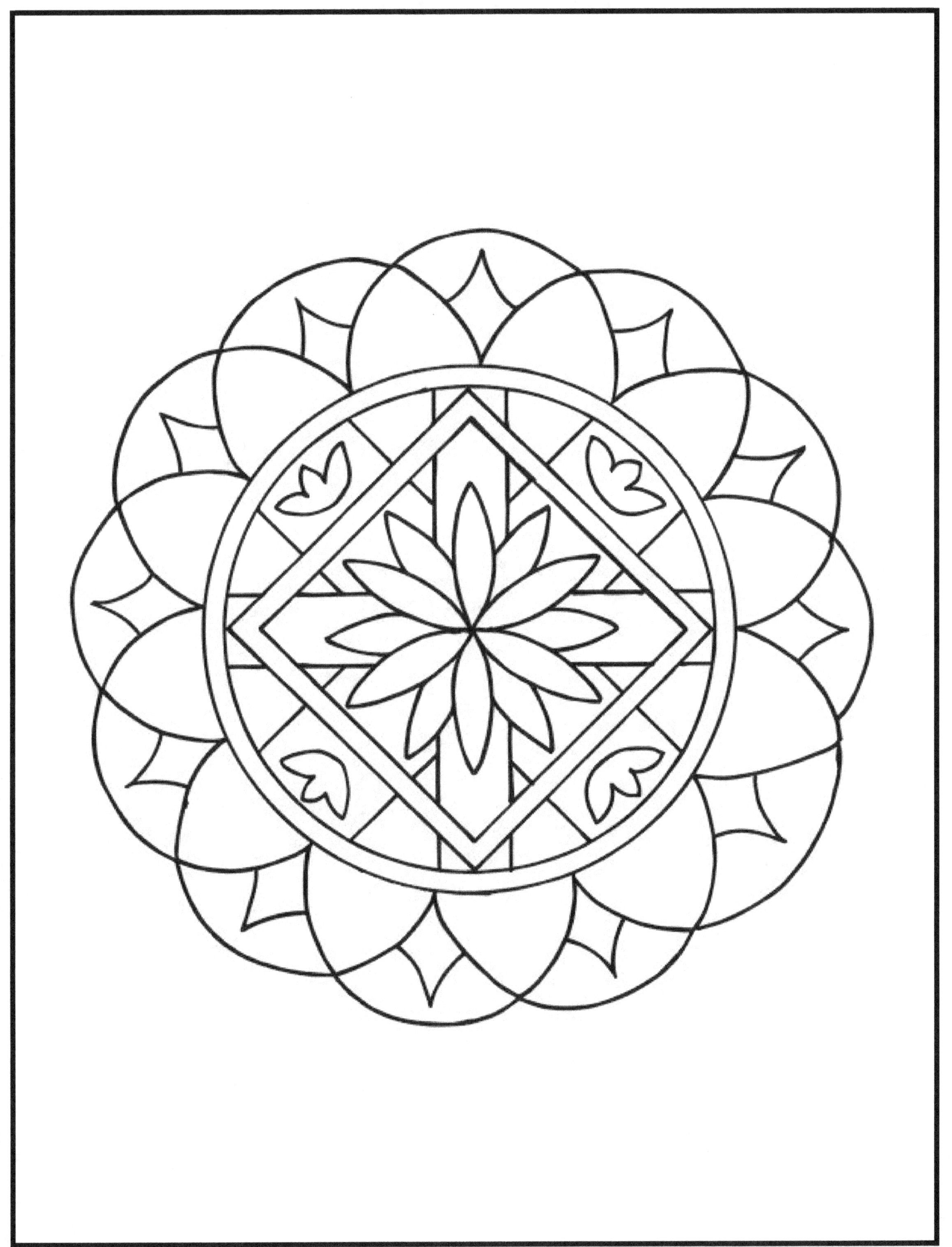

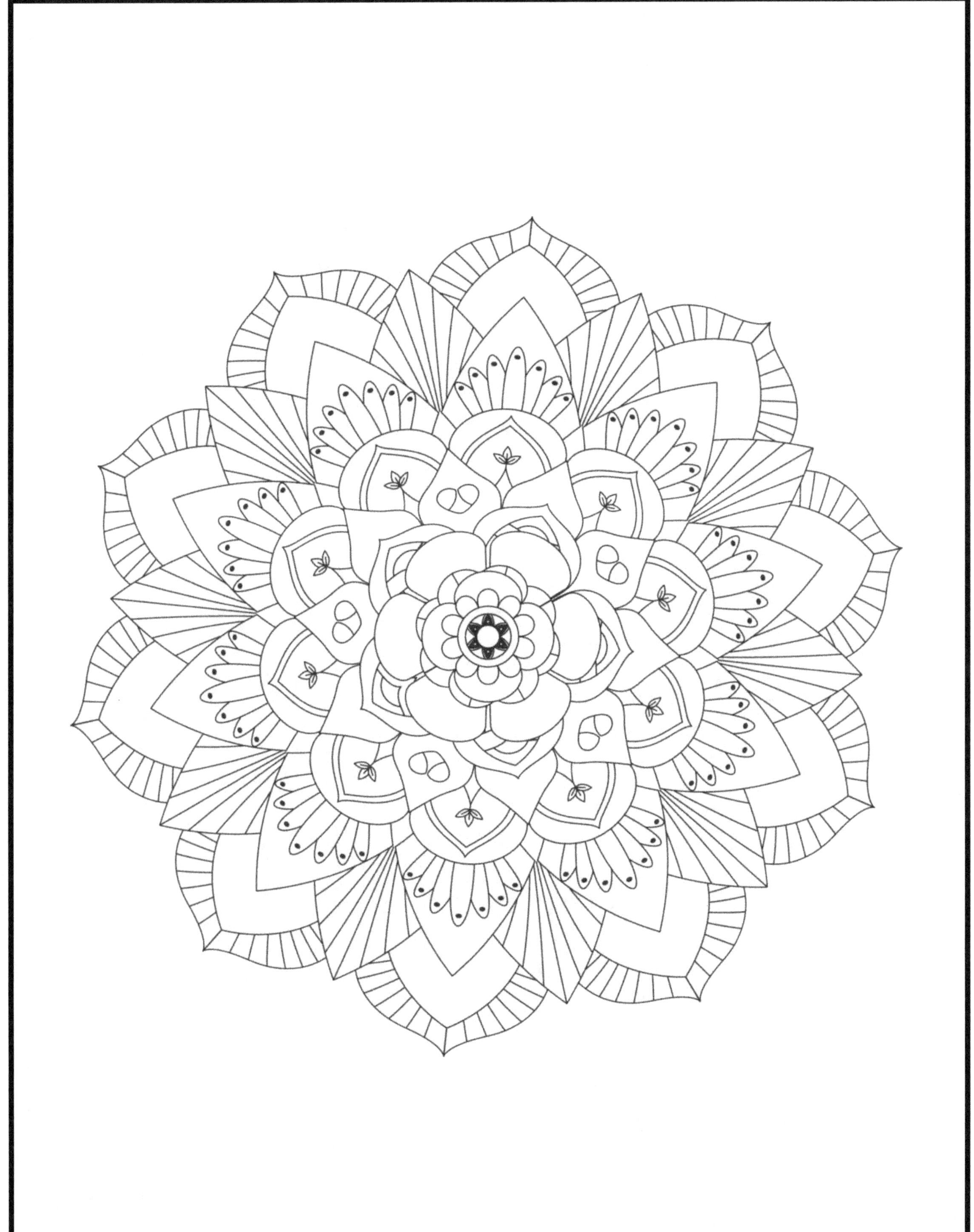

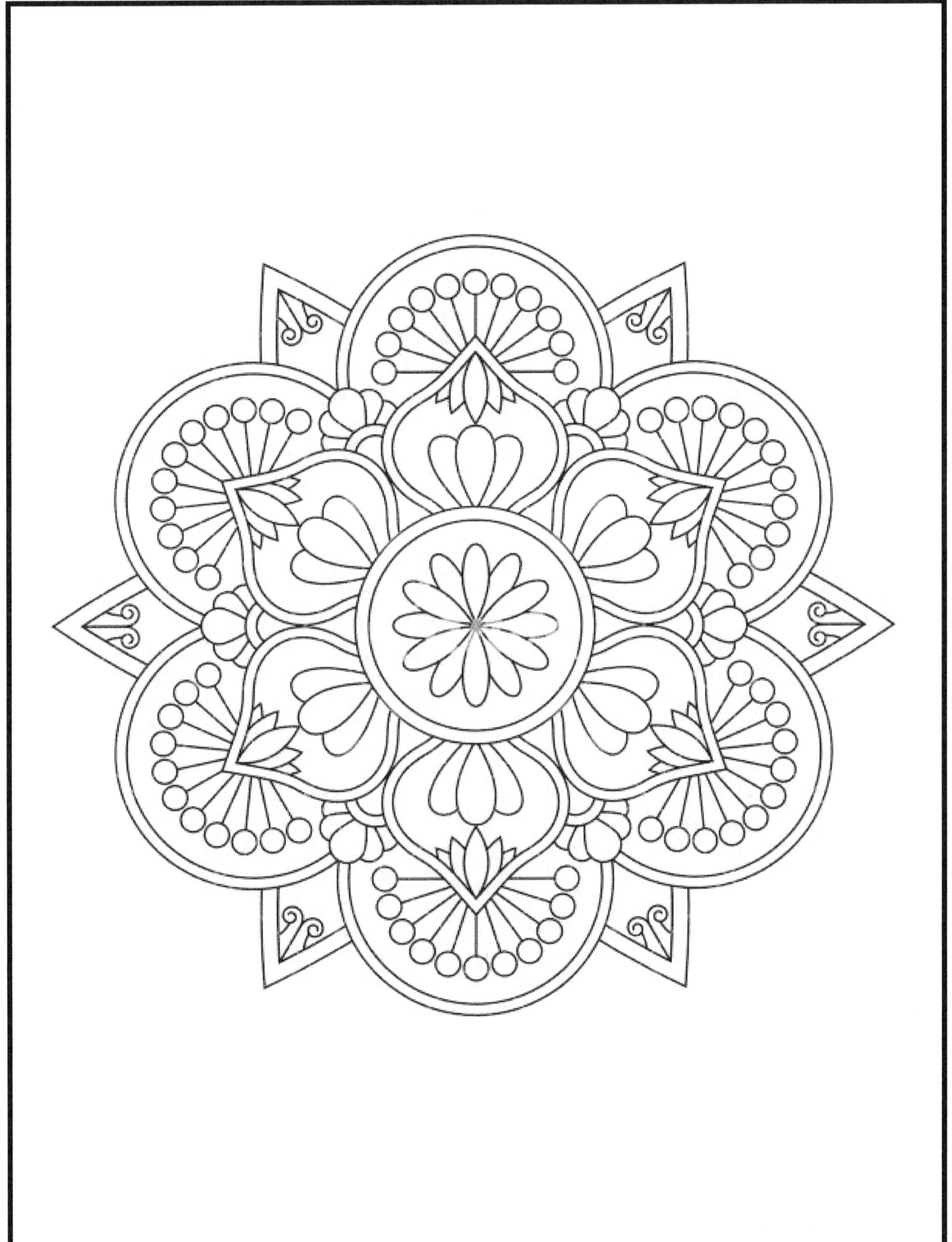

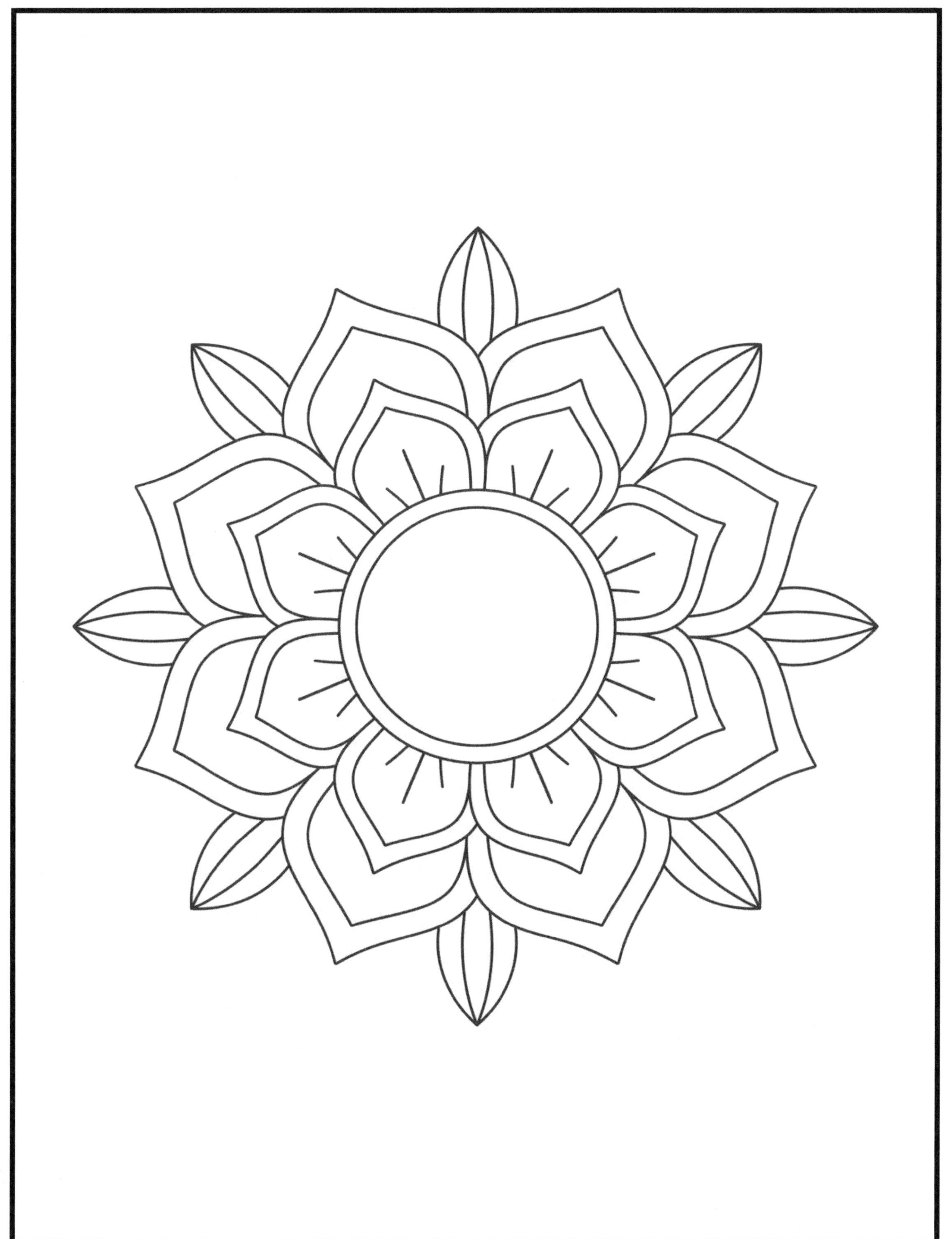

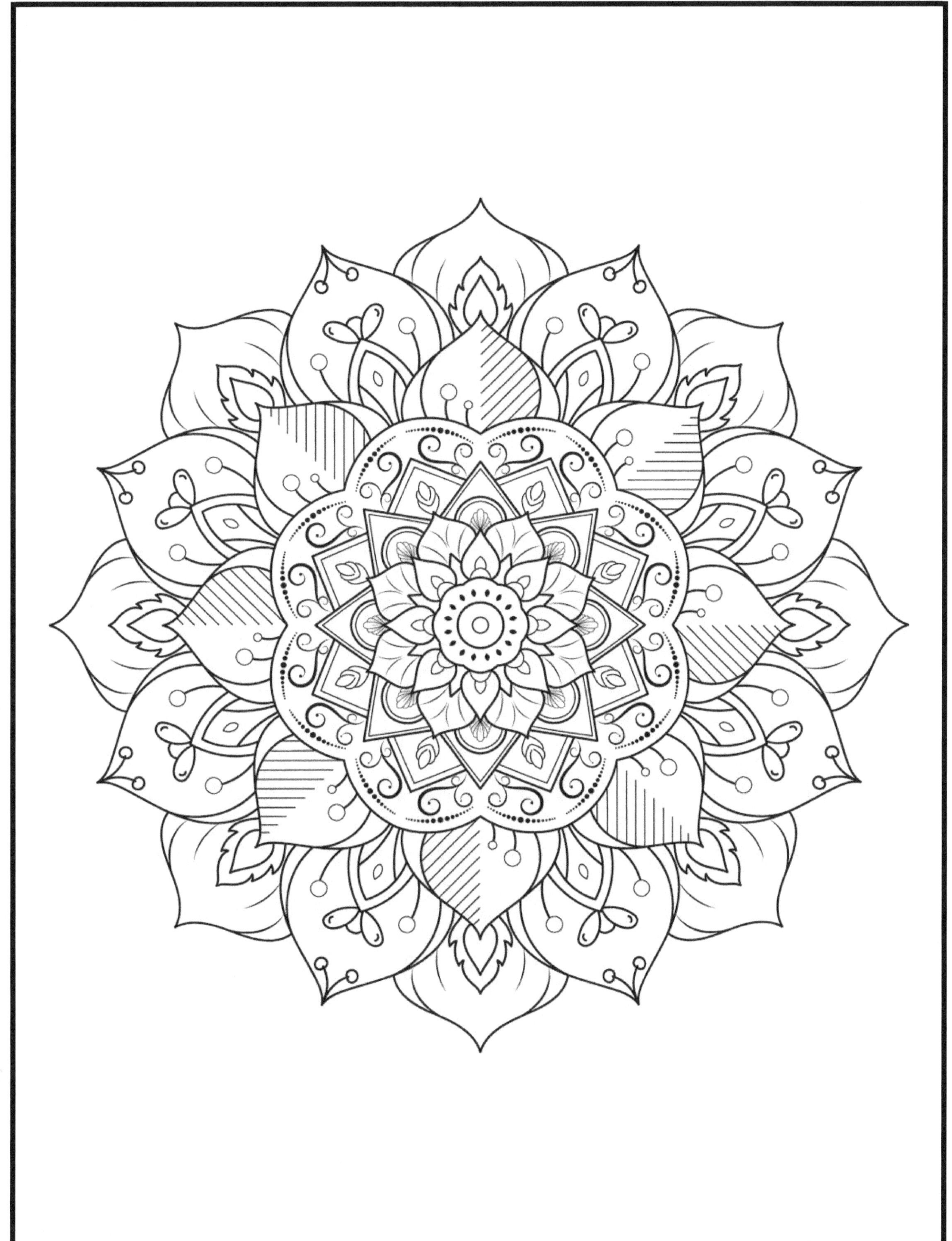

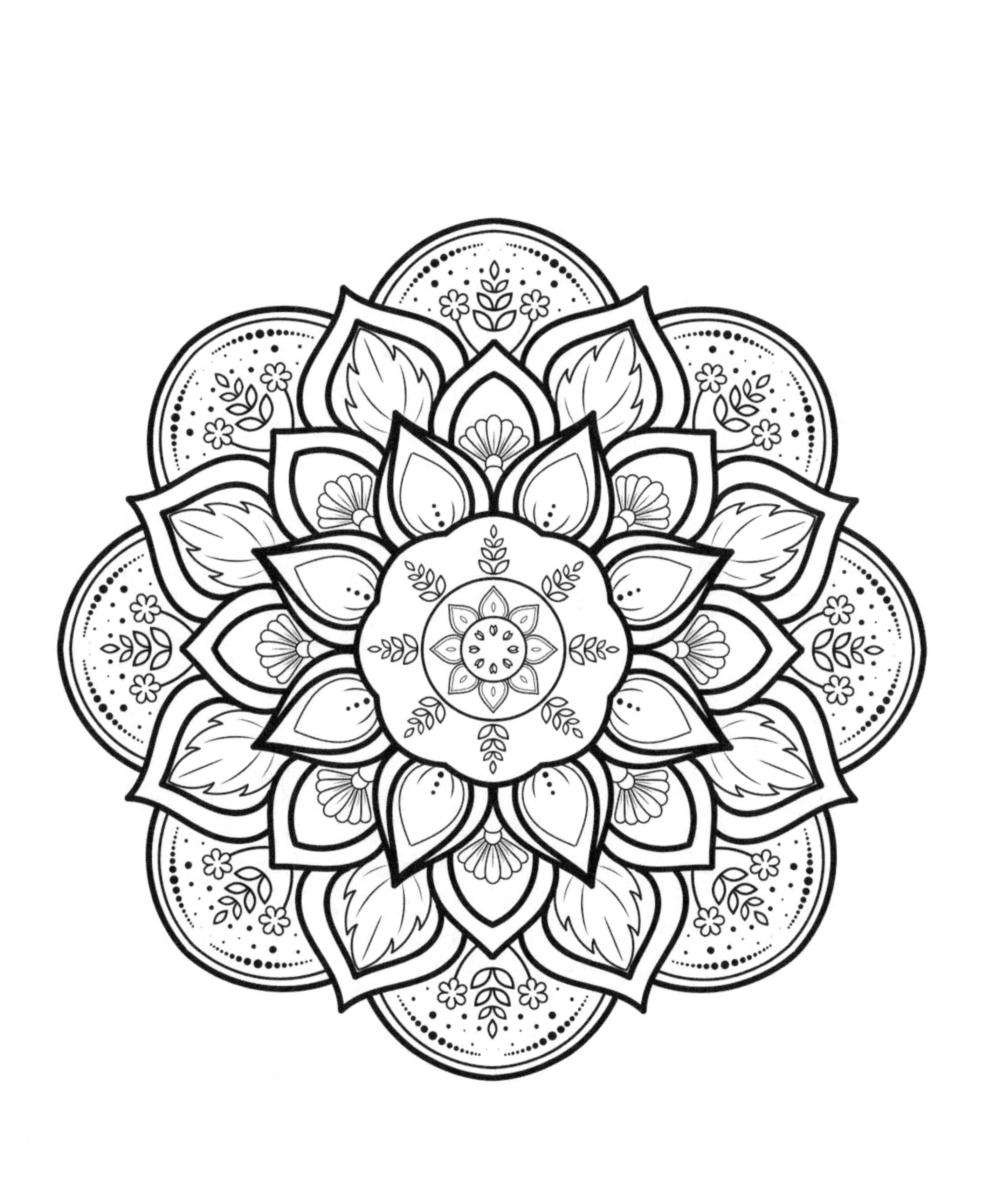

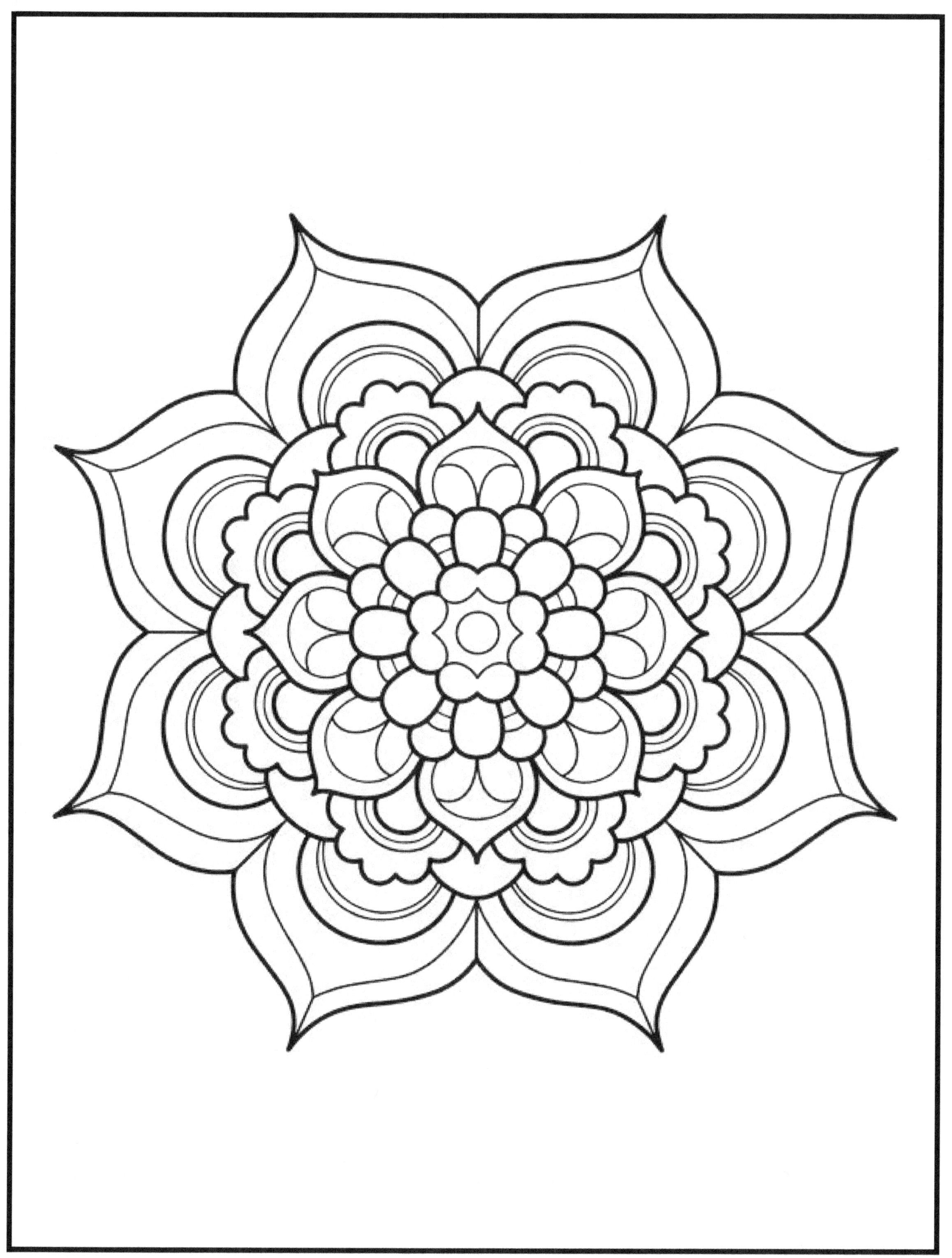

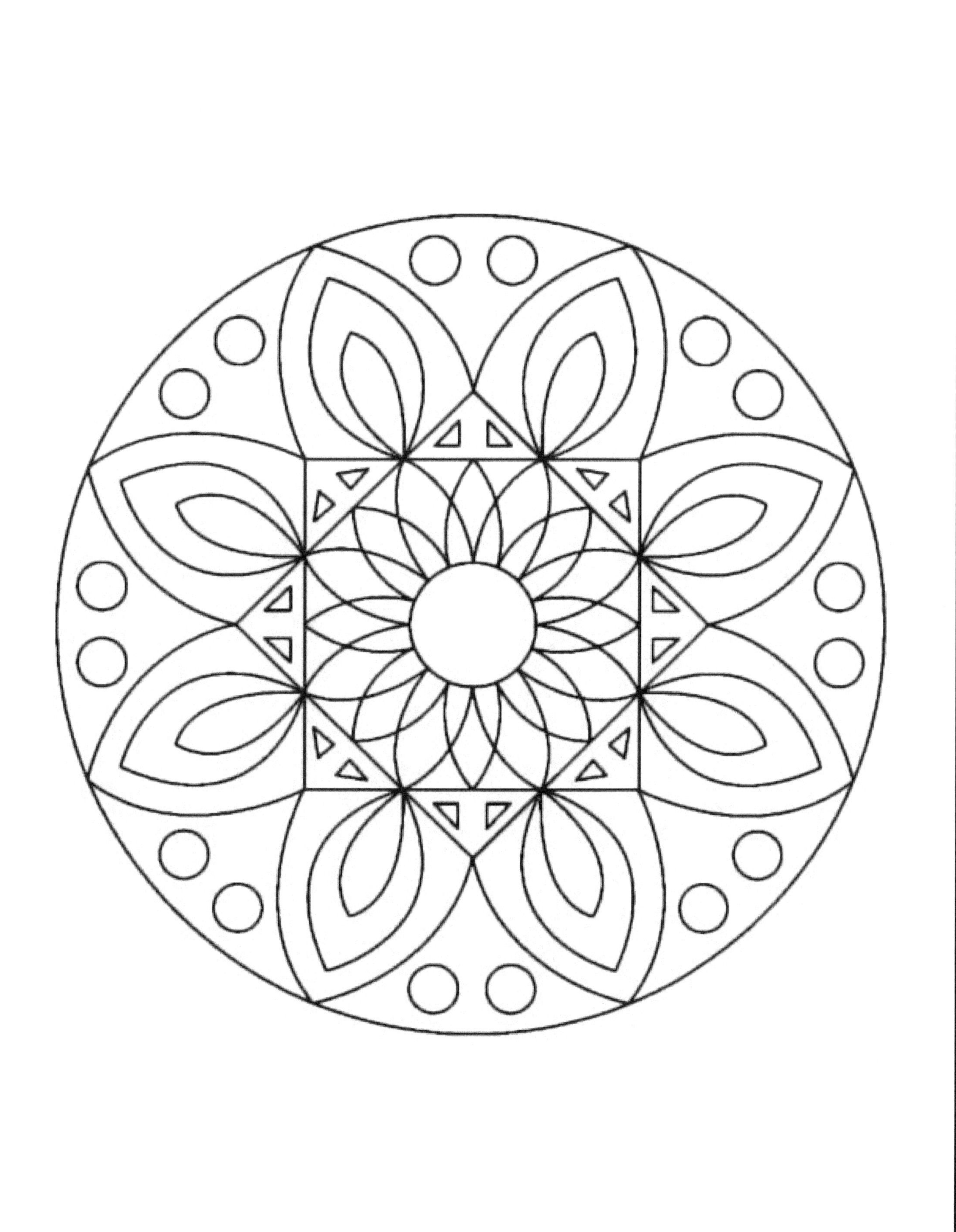

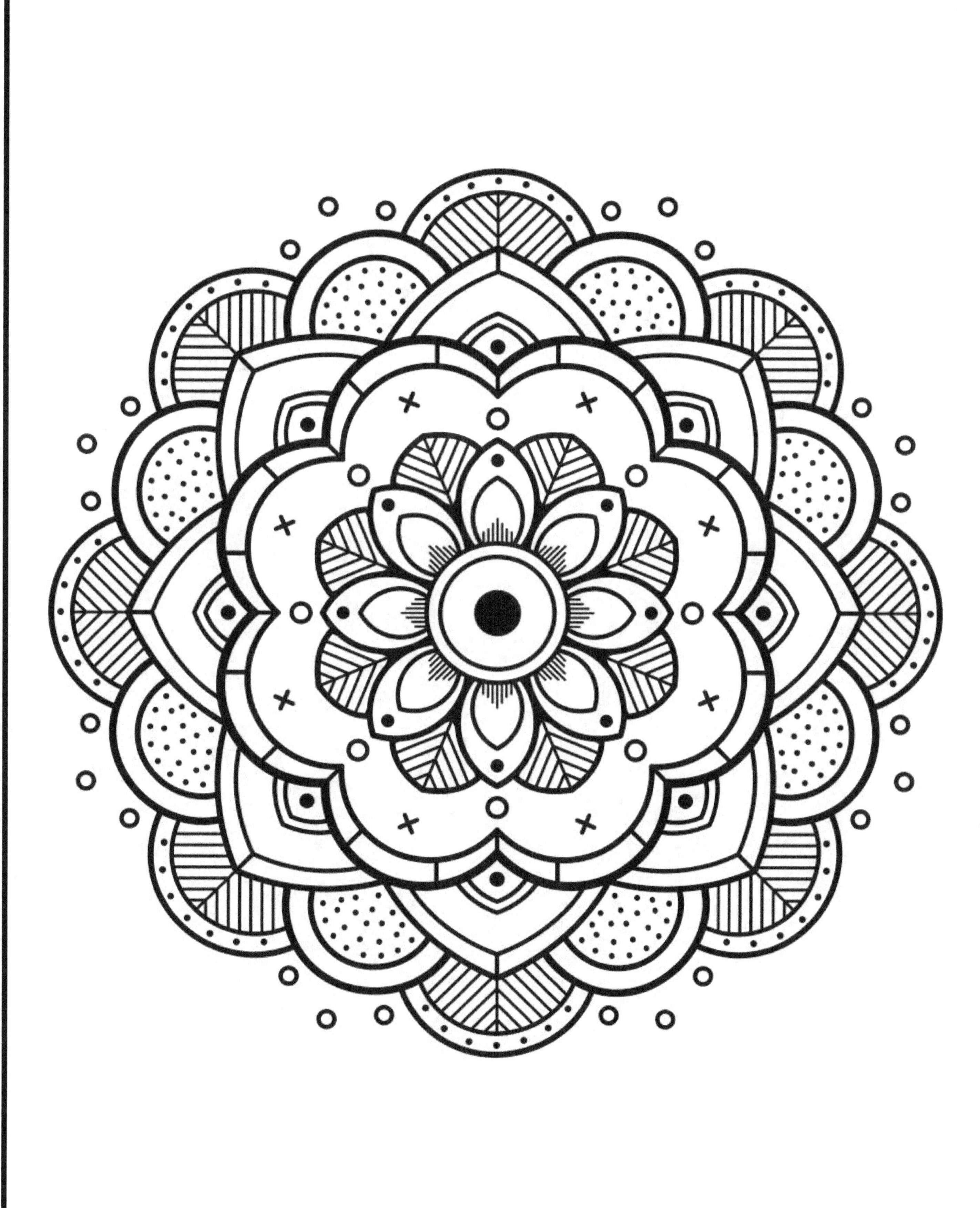

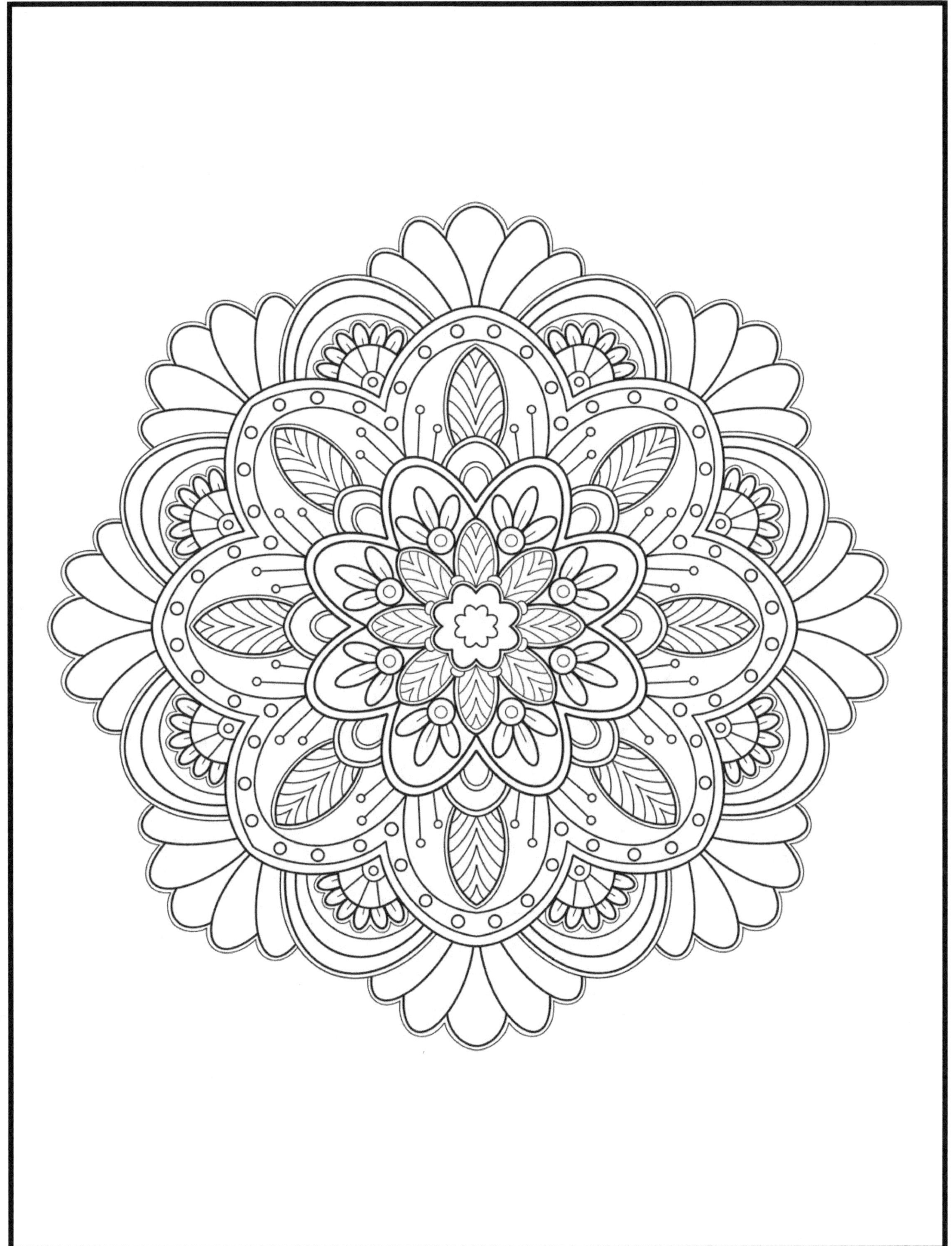

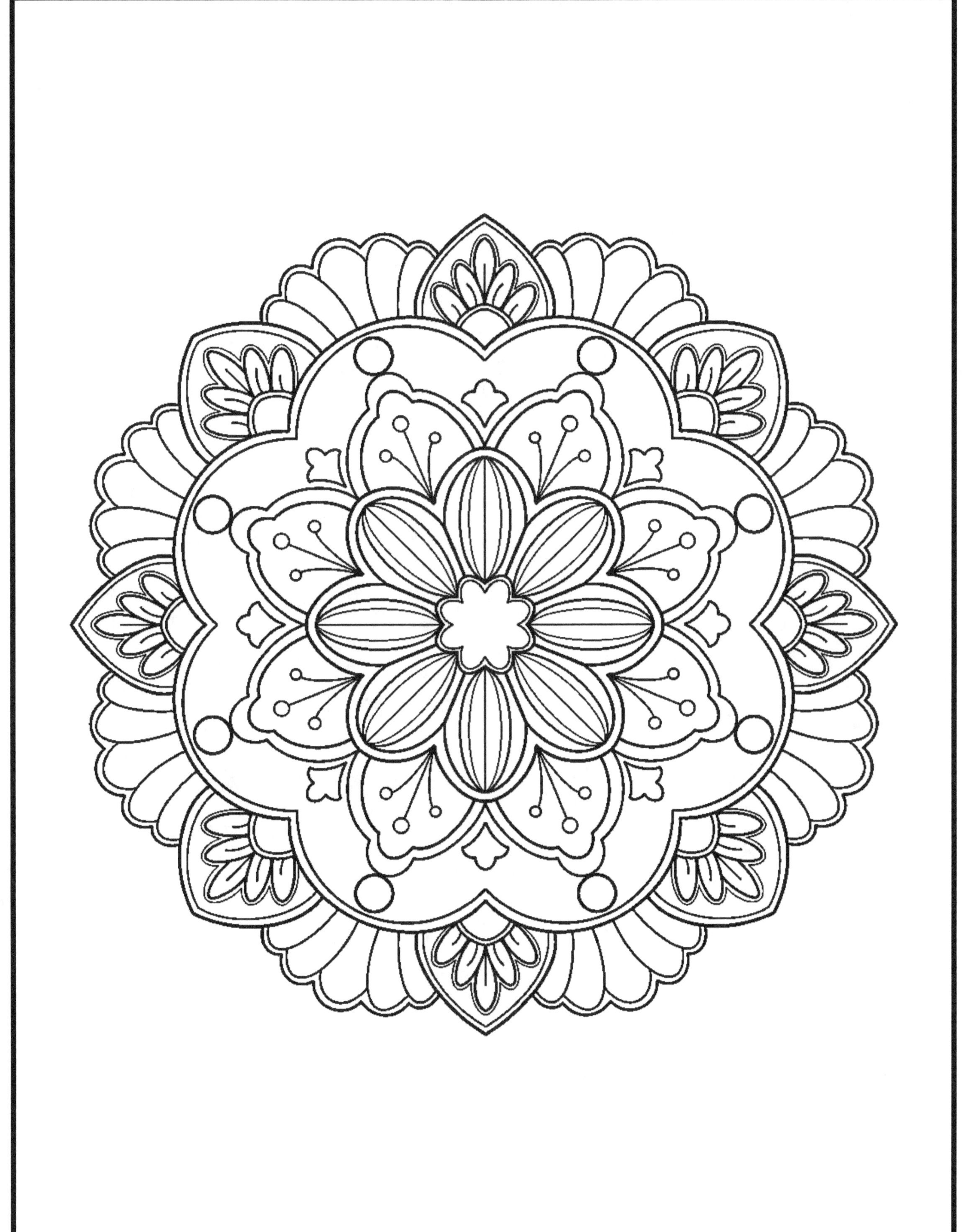

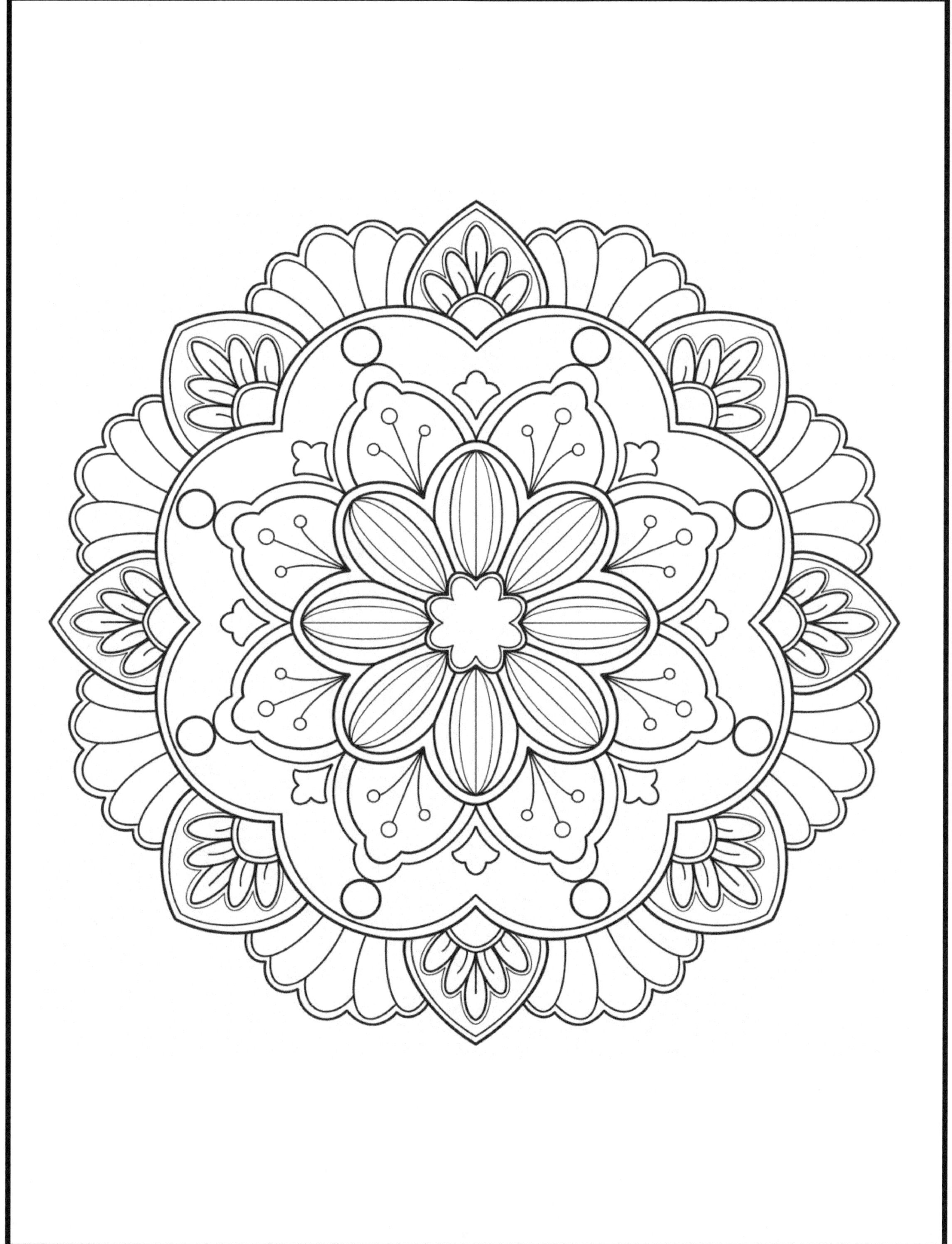

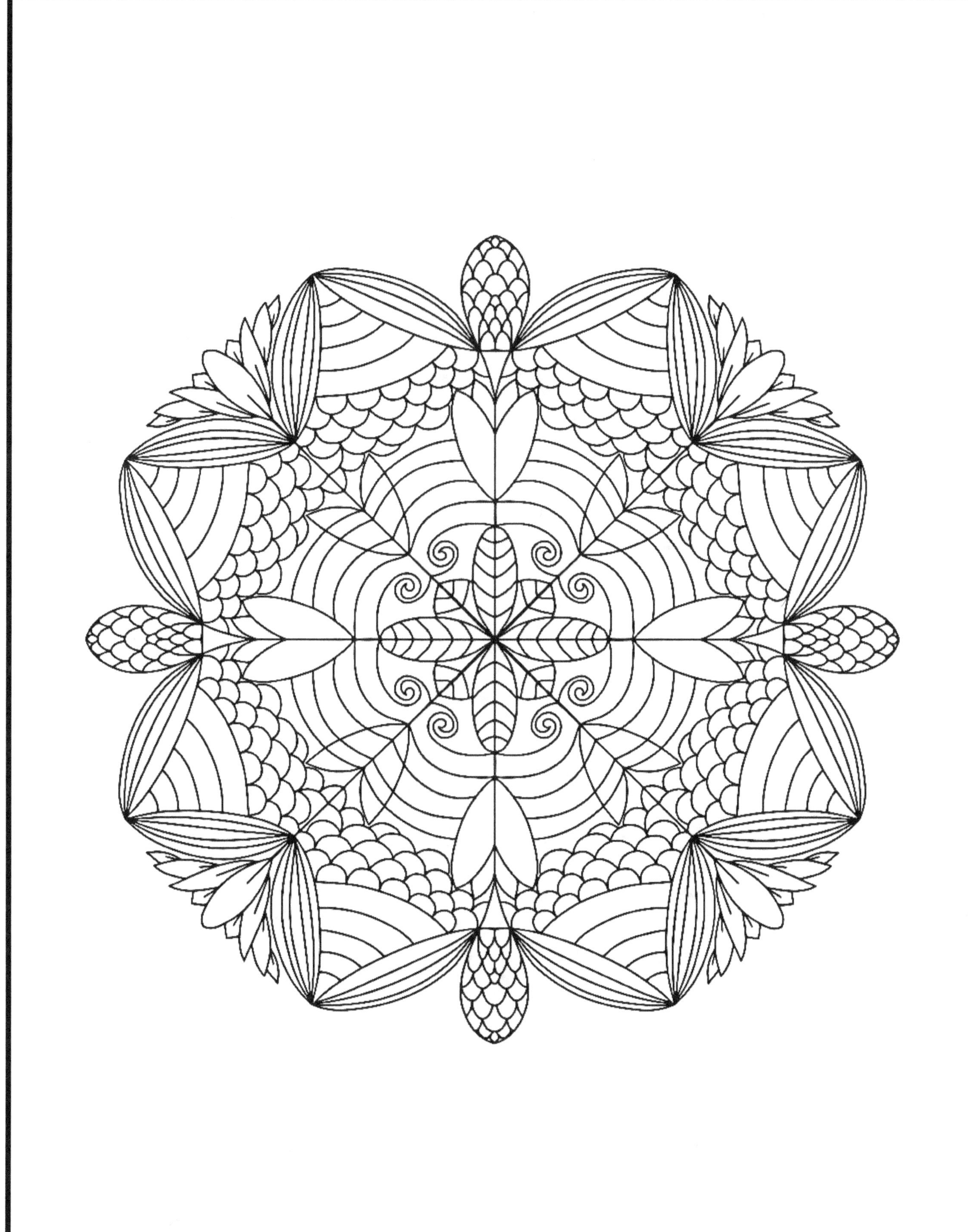

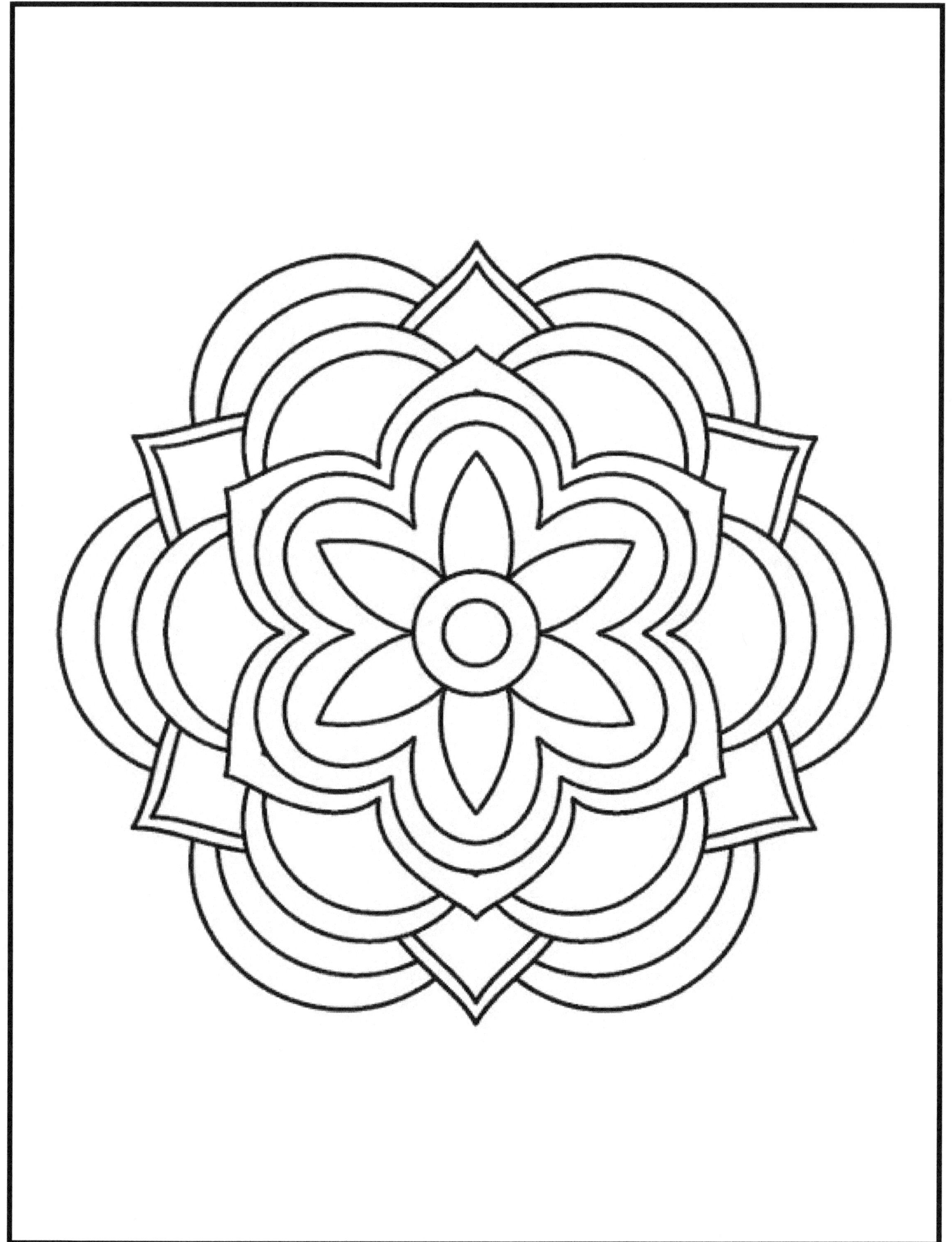

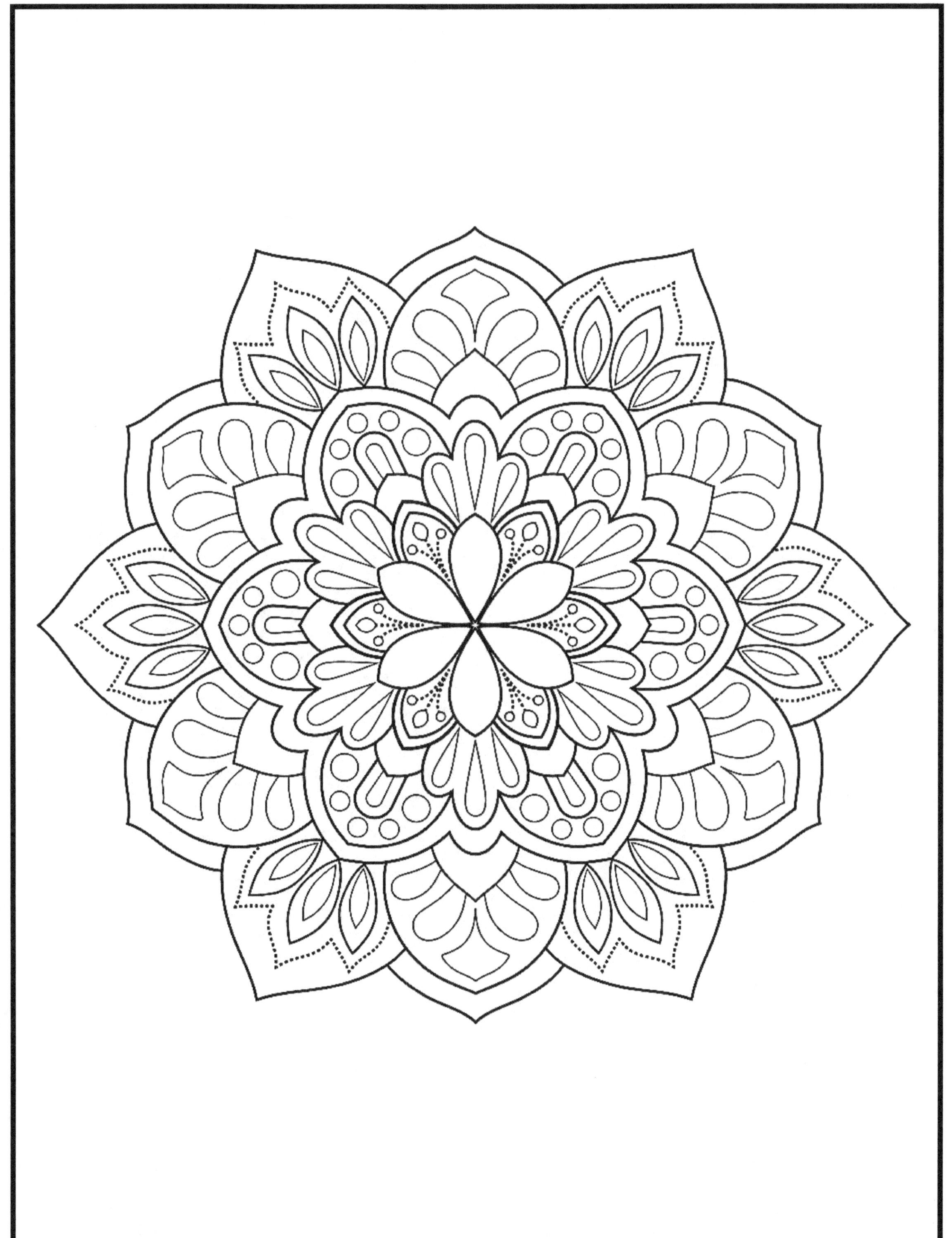

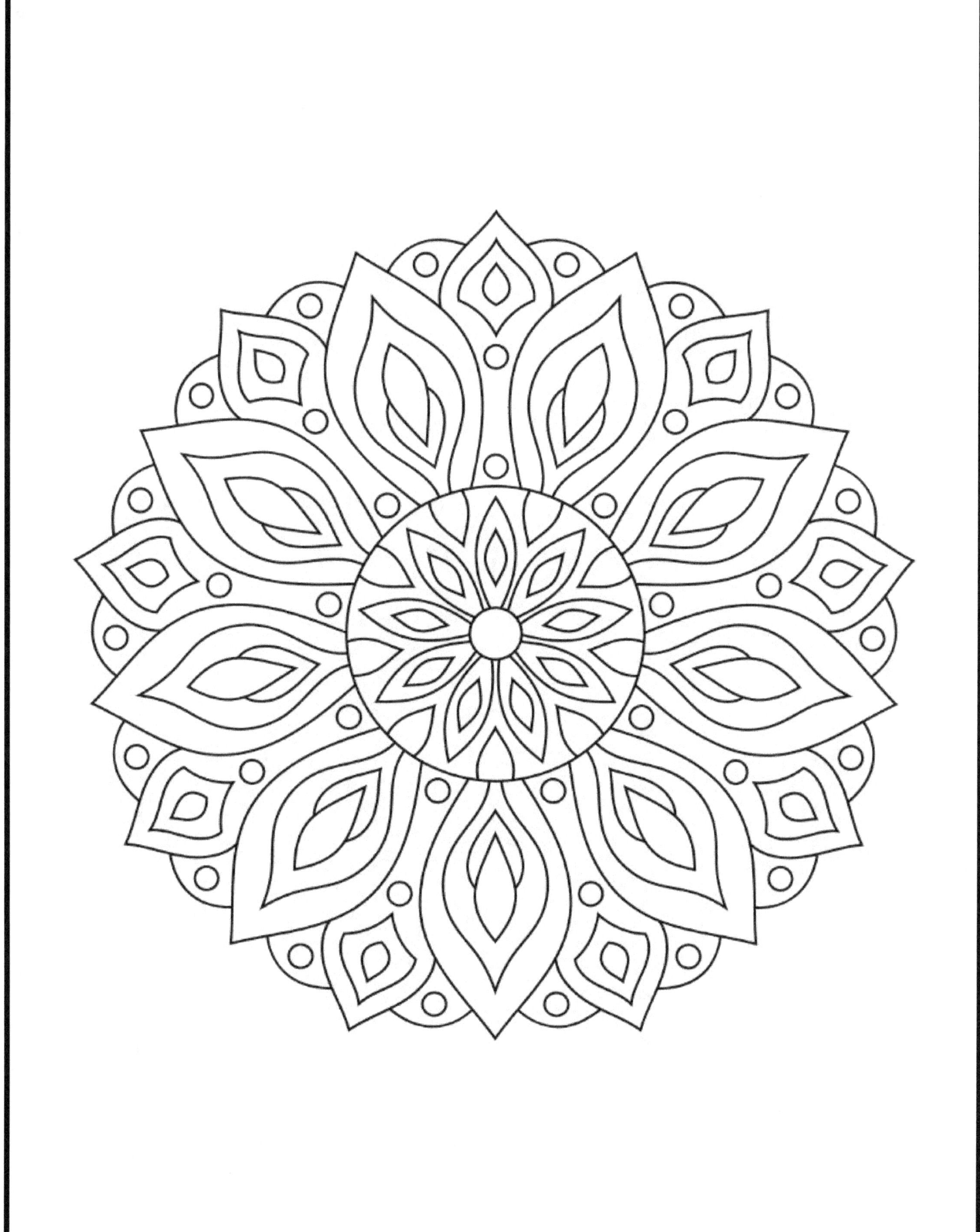

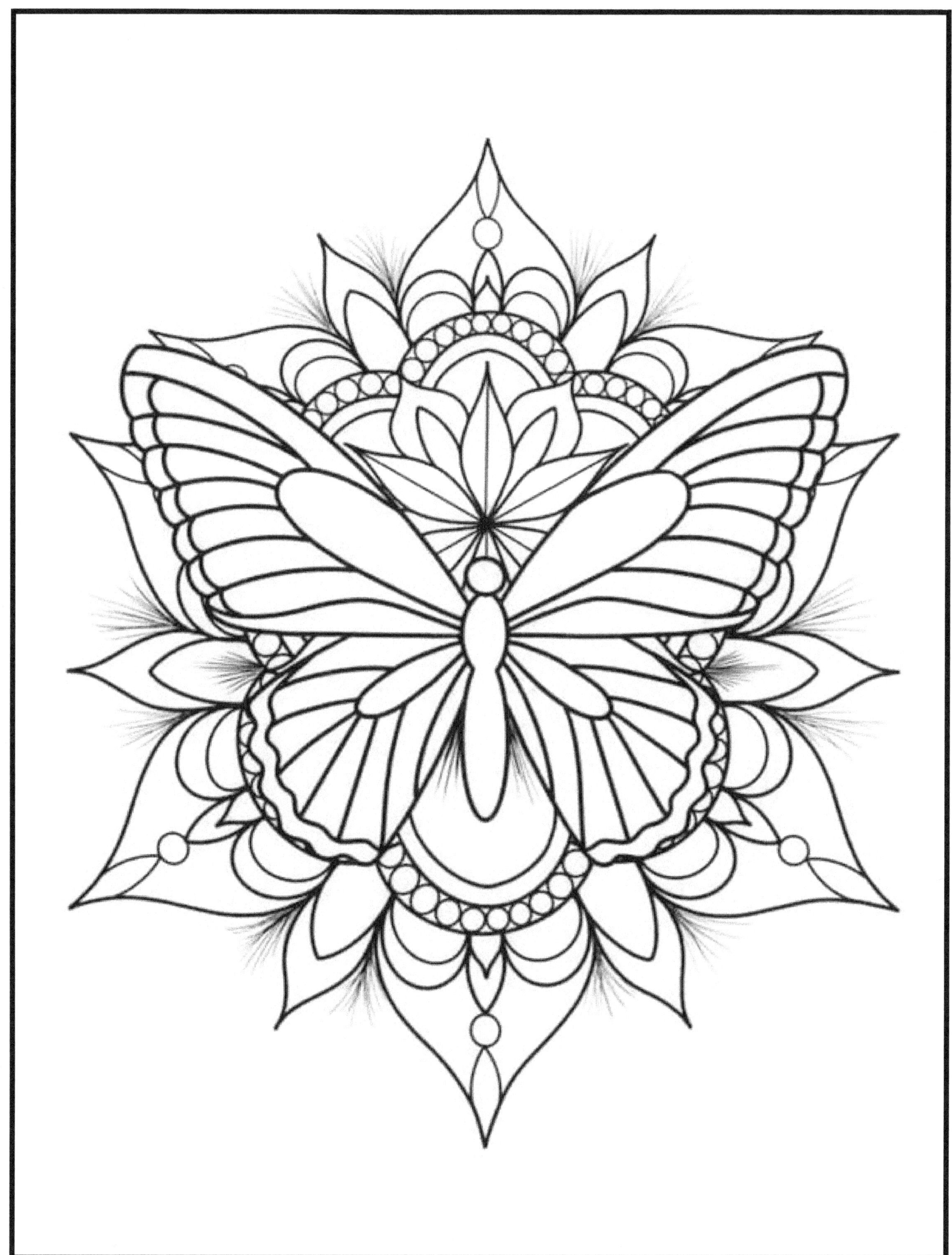

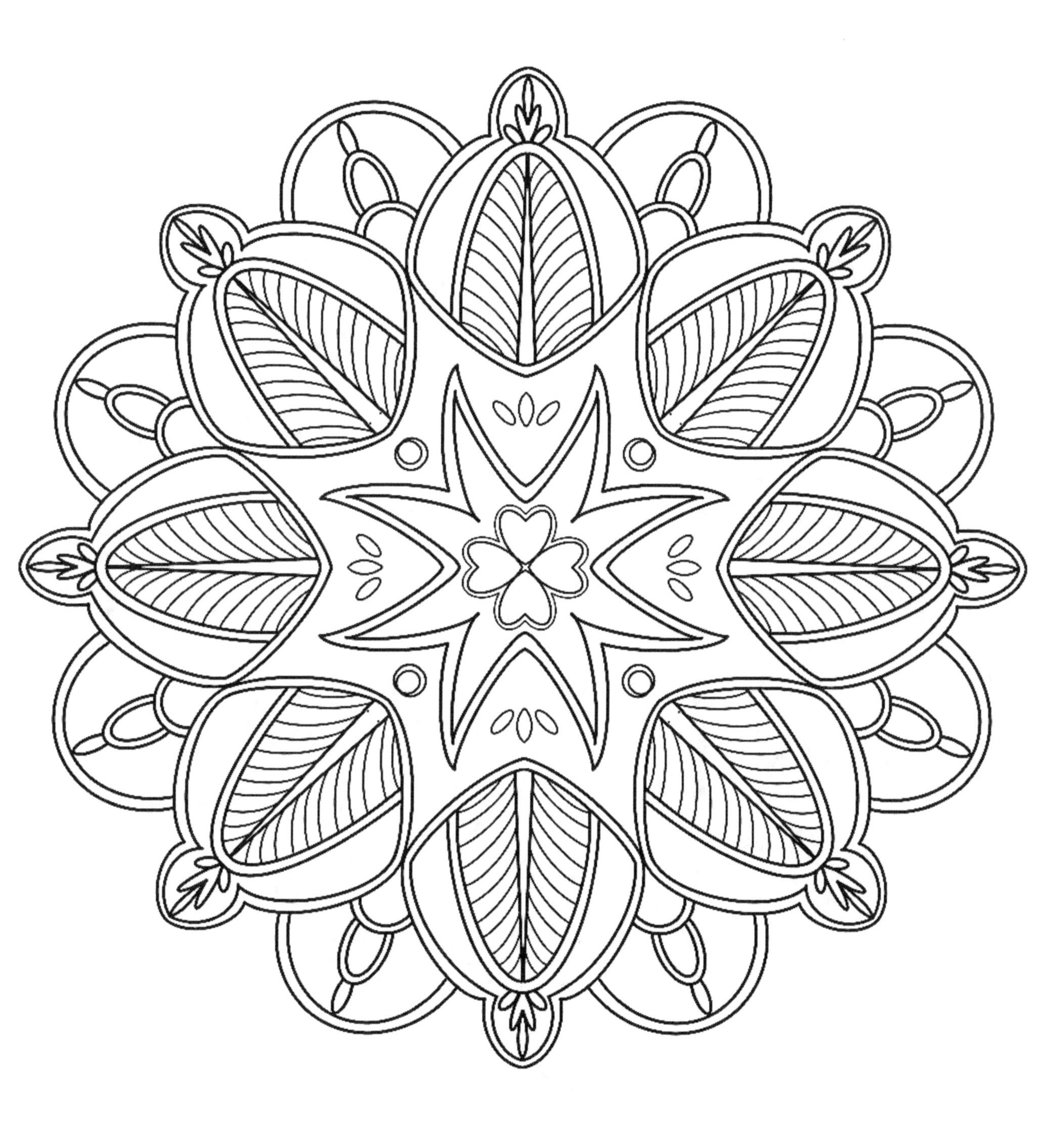

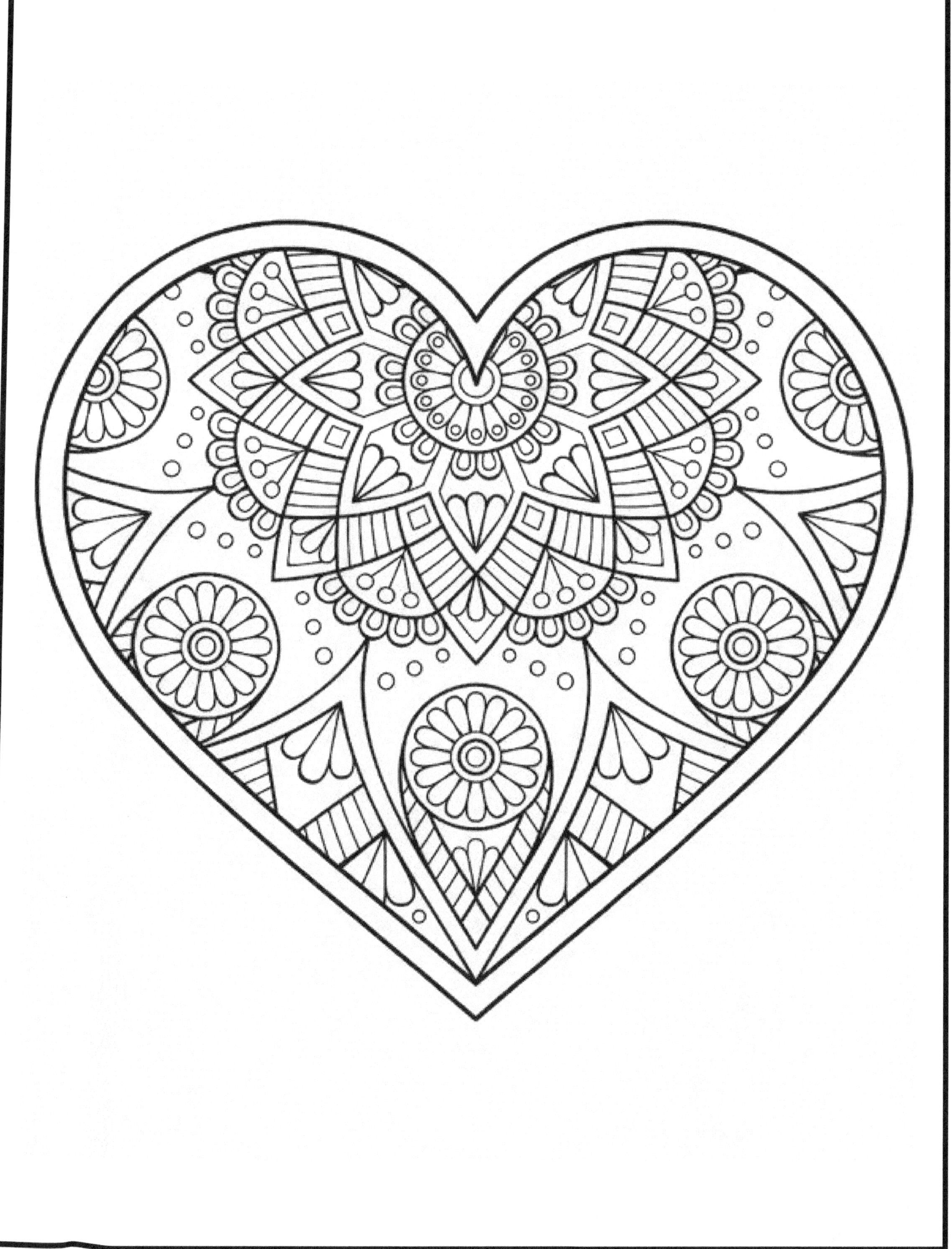